Introduction to
Clothing Manufacture

Introduction to Clothing Manufacture

Gerry Cooklin

Second Edition revised by
Steven G. Hayes
John McLoughlin

Blackwell
Science

© 2006 S.G. Hayes, J. McLoughlin and the Estate of Gerry Cooklin.

Blackwell Publishing Ltd
Editorial offices:
Blackwell Science Ltd, 9600 Garsington Road, Oxford OX4 2DQ, UK
  Tel: +44 (0) 1865 776868
Blackwell Publishing Professional, 2121 State Avenue, Ames, Iowa 50014-8300, USA
  Tel: +1 515 292 0140
Blackwell Science Asia Pty Ltd, 550 Swanston Street, Carlton, Victoria 3053, Australia
  Tel: +61 (0)3 8359 1011

First edition published 1991
Second edition published 2006 by Blackwell Publishing

ISBN-10: 0-632-05846-3
ISBN-13: 978-0-632-05846-4

Library of Congress Cataloging-in-Publication Data
Cooklin, Gerry.
Introduction to clothing manufacture/Gerry Cooklin; second edition revised by Steven G. Hayes, John McLoughlin. – 2nd ed.
    p. cm.
Includes bibliographical references and index.
ISBN-13: 978-0-632-05846-4 (pbk. : alk. paper)
ISBN-10: 0-632-05846-3 (pbk. : alk. paper)
1. Clothing trade. 2. Clothing factories. I. Hayes, Steven G., 1970– II. McLoughlin, John (John Joseph) III. Title.
TT497.C67 2006
687′.04–dc22
2005035497

A catalogue record for this title is available from the British Library

Set in 10/12.5pt Sabon
by SNP Best-set Typesetter Ltd., Hong Kong

FSC
Mixed Sources
Product group from well-managed
forests and other controlled sources
Cert no. SGS-COC-2953
www.fsc.org
© 1996 Forest Stewardship Council

For further information on Blackwell Publishing, visit our website:
www.blackwellpublishing.com

Contents

Preface

As with the first edition, the objective of this book is to provide an introductory and panoramic view of the managerial and technological factors which influence the day to day operations of a clothing manufacturer. Yet, since the publication of the first edition in 1991, there has been continual change to the global distribution of this still-vibrant industry. From a localised perspective, it is easy to see the industry only in the negative light of factory closures and the migration of manufacturing. However, this offers new opportunities and adventures to those people engaging in the fashion business. To this end, we have attempted to bring some sections of the book up to date with recent developments: for example, by giving an indication of the cost to manufacture in the countries now involved in the global supply of fashion goods; the new technologies involved in joining textile materials together; the need to reconsider how manufacturing technologies are exploited; emerging trends in garment transportation; and, covering all of this, the quality management issues facing a globally distributed supply chain. We hope we have done this while keeping the integrity of Gerry's first edition and yet adding our own interpretation of the current environment. If we can reiterate the statement in the original preface:

> 'No single book can provide a completely comprehensive and in-depth explanation of all the factors involved in the design, marketing and production of clothing. Many of the topics are the subject of specialist literature, to which readers should refer for any extensive studies. The book does provide a useful foundation for advanced study and will be helpful as a practical reference tool for the future.'

We wish you luck with your endeavours in the fashion business and hope that this book can help in some small way.

Steve Hayes and John McLoughlin

Introduction

While the way we talk about the 'fashion business' now reflects the transformation of a traditional, locally based, production-centred industry into a creative and knowledge-based feeder for a consumer-centric retailing business, it is important to acknowledge that the essence of clothing manufacture has changed less than is suggested in the new language that we use. Fabric still needs to be cut, although this is now commonly done with computer-controlled bladed cutters (or is perhaps even laser cut) rather than by hand with straight knives; it still needs to be joined together, still predominantly by sewing but also now using non-sewn techniques; and finally, it still needs to be packaged and distributed. Indeed, because clothing manufacturing is essentially still a labour-intensive process and because of the consumer-centric nature of the modern retail environment, it is increasingly important that the resources employed be managed effectively. This need is compounded by the global nature of the fashion business.

The cost of direct labour, and the consumer's desire for value, have worked together over the last 20 years to drive production to lower and lower cost production centres (see Table 1.5, p. 6). At the time of writing this second edition, it is difficult to ignore the rise of China to the position of 'the factory of the world'. Other dominant manufacturing centres include India, Sri Lanka and Turkey – but where next? In time, it is possible that South America and even sub-Saharan Africa (with improved stability and health) will be the main suppliers of manufactured goods to the consuming world. Wherever the products are made, the principles outlined in this book apply: whether we talk about 'fast fashion' for the fashion business or 'making clothes', the effective management of people, materials and time is at the centre of an efficient enterprise.

Acknowledgements

The help and support of the following are gratefully acknowledged:

Manchester Metropolitan University, Department of Clothing Design and Technology: Michael Jeffrey, Anita Mitchell, Tina Wallace and Neville Haynes

William Lee Innovation Centre, Textiles and Paper, School of Materials, University of Manchester: Dr Tilak Dias, Head of the William Lee Innovation Centre, Dr Richard Kennon, Tony Nuttall, Simon Reynolds, Johanna Bergvall-Forsberg, Jo Lambert, Umair Saeed and Pete Wilcock

David Mellett and Ian Butcher, Matalan PLC

Cecille Harari-Alle, Lectra UK Ltd, cutting, pattern and grading systems

Stuart Barker, Sabre Sewing Machines, Stockport, Manchester

Celia Thornley, Skillfast-UK, the sector skills council for apparel, footwear, textiles and related businesses

Part 1
THE CLOTHING INDUSTRY

1 Structure of the Clothing Industry

Size structure

Entry to the clothing manufacturing industry has always been easy because of the relatively small amount of capital required to purchase machinery and the necessary raw materials, and the availability of relatively low cost and low skilled labour (increasingly scarce in the economically developed nations). For over a century the industry has been dominated by one simple, cheap and long-lived tool, the basic sewing machine, and this not only facilitates entry into the industry but virtually dictates its structure. This is amply demonstrated by the large number of small factories which exist within the industry.

A study specific to the UK clothing industry conducted in 1996 illustrates this view (2). Table 1.1 is an extract showing enterprises of fewer than 100 employees accounting for 97.7% of all enterprises, 52.2% of all those employed, 47.7% of gross output and 46.6% of net output.

What should be of interest to the reader is the fact that in the original edition of this book a 1971 survey of the clothing industry within the European Economic Community (now, of course, the EU) also showed the preponderance of small factories (25). So we see that although the global activity of the industry may be more dispersed and the nature of the products being made more varied, there is still a high level of reliance upon small manufacturers which has remained through a period of consolidation in other manufacturing industries such as automotive, chemical and materials. At that time, the total number of people employed by the EEC clothing industries was 1 608 500 and they were dispersed over 26 500 factories, with the distribution shown in Table 1.2.

Small factories employing up to 25 people represented 44% of the total number of factories in the industry, and in themselves these small factories accounted for a substantial percentage of the total clothing production, especially where fashion merchandise was concerned. However, the bulk of clothing production, as measured by the number of employees, was concentrated in factories that had more than 100 employees, as shown in Table 1.3.

According to this table, nearly 50% of the people working in the EEC clothing industry were employed in large factories having over 100 employees. The total

Table 1.1 Basic size distribution (%) of UK apparel (division 18) manufacturing industry (2). Reproduced with permission

Size category	ENT	EMP	GO	NO
1–9	71.9	20.4		
10–19	13.6	8.6	47.7	46.6
20–49	9.1	13.1		
50–99	3.1	10.1		
100–199	1.1	7.7	7.2	6.9
200–299	0.5	5.6	5.6	5.0
300–399	0.2	2.7	2.8	2.6
400–499	0.1	3.1	3.8	3.7
500–749	0.2	7.1	9.9	9.8
750–999	0.1	3.8	4.7	4.9
1000–1499	0.1	3.0	3.0	3.1
1500–1999	0.1	4.6	7.0	9.1
2000	0.1	10.1	8.2	8.2

ENT = enterprises; EMP = employment; GO = gross output; NO = net output.

Table 1.2 Distribution of factories according to employees

Employees	Factories
1–25	11 660
26–50	8 480
51–100	3 630
Over 100	2 730

Table 1.3 Distribution of employees according to factories

Number of employees	Total employed
1–25	212 323
26–50	294 355
51–100	310 440
Over 100	791 382

structure of the EEC clothing industry at the time of the survey was as shown in Table 1.4.

Manufacturing structure

The clothing industry manufactures an enormous variety of garment types ranging from work clothes to ball gowns, and the production itself can be carried out by one of two types of organisation: a manufacturer or a sub-contractor. This model

Table 1.4 Distribution of employees and factories (see also Fig. 1.1)

Number of factories	Average number of employees
110 660	18
8 480	34
3 330	85
2 730	290

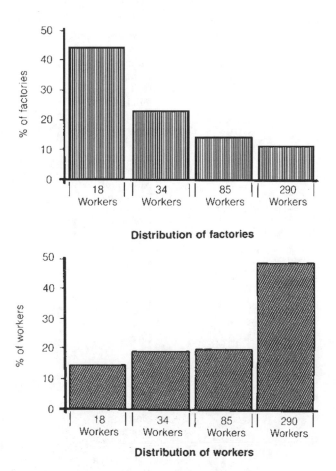

Fig. 1.1 Distribution of workers and factories (EEC 1971)

of production is further complicated by the relationship with a retailer (the public face of the clothing industry) where a retailer can work directly with a manufacturer, or even be part of the same company; interact with a manufacturer through a sourcing agent; or buy products from a wholesale distributor. Whatever form the manufacturing organisation takes, it is likely to be globally dispersed, with the assembly stages (and varying amounts of the other functions) located in low labour cost countries. Indeed the disparity between labour costs (Table 1.5) can be

Table 1.5 Hourly labour costs worldwide in US dollars (including on-costs), 1998. Data kindly supplied by Werner International

Geographic group	Rate	Geographic group	Rate
NAFTA		*Other European*	
USA	10.12	Bulgaria	n/a
Canada	9.89	Norway	18.23
Mexico	1.34	Romania	1.04
		Russia	0.56
Central America		Switzerland	17.56
Costa Rica	2.52	Turkey	1.84
Dominican Republic	1.48		
El Salvador	1.35	*Asia/Asia-Pacific*	
Guatemala	0.91	Australia	9.41
Haiti	n/a	Bangladesh	0.30
Honduras	1.28	Cambodia	0.20
Jamaica	n/a	Hong Kong	5.20
Nicaragua	n/a	India	0.39
		Indonesia	0.16
South America		Japan	13.55
Argentina	3.66	South Korea	2.69
Bolivia	n/a	Malaysia	1.30
Brazil	2.03	Myanmar	0.13
Chile	2.37	New Zealand	5.19
Columbia	1.27	Pakistan	0.24
Paraguay	n/a	Philippines	0.76
Peru	1.46	People's Republic of China	0.43
Uruguay	3.00	Singapore	n/a
Venezuela	2.57	Sri Lanka	0.44
		Taiwan	4.68
European Union		Thailand	0.78
Austria	14.32	Vietnam	0.22
Belgium	16.49		
Czech Republic	1.65	*Middle East and Africa*	
Denmark	18.71	Algeria	n/a
Estonia	1.34	Egypt	0.68
Finland	13.96	Ethiopia	0.27
France	13.03	Israel	5.37
Germany	18.04	Kenya	0.34
Greece	6.55	Madagascar	0.31
Hungary	2.12	Mauritius	1.03
Ireland	8.72	Morocco	1.36
Italy	13.60	Nigeria	0.69
Malta	5.54	Oman	1.89
Netherlands	14.71	South Africa	1.39
Poland	2.77	Tunisia	n/a
Portugal	3.70	Zambia	0.36
Slovakia	1.30		
Spain	6.79		
Sweden	16.30		
UK	10.86		

considered the main driver in the globalisation of the clothing manufacturing industry. While many arguments have been constructed to suggest that the benefits of producing in low labour cost countries are overestimated, it is difficult to argue against the evidence of many organisations in the higher labour cost countries mutating into a new form of clothing provider – a sourcing company. Taking as an example the disparity between labour costs for the UK and for the People's Republic of China (10.86 and 0.43 US$/hr respectively), it is easy to see why what is still essentially a labour-intensive production process has migrated to countries with such low labour costs.

Manufacturer on own account

This is the type of organisation which is responsible for every stage in the production of garments, from design and selling to production and deliveries to the customer. The strength of this type of organisation lies in design and marketing expertise and the ability to:

- anticipate or follow very closely the changes in fashion;
- anticipate possible fluctuations in the level of demand;
- finance the operation of the business.

Sub-contractors

These account for most of the small factories within the clothing industry and they exist because they produce garments of acceptable quality at competitive prices in a short throughput time. The contractor's prices must not only be competitive with those of other sub-contractors, but must also be low enough to make it attractive for the manufacturer to produce via the sub-contractor, rather than to produce for himself. The strength of the sub-contractor is in factory management and the maintenance of very low overheads. In addition he must:

- maintain continuity of production;
- ensure that his customers are reputable and financially secure;
- recognise and select the most profitable opportunities;
- obtain high productivity levels from the labour force;
- utilise to the full all the materials supplied by the manufacturer.

As an individual, the sub-contractor will perform nearly all the management and administrative functions within the factory and will also regularly visit the manufacturers supplying work to the unit. The exception to the typical small sub-contractor can be found in the Asia/Asia Pacific region where the largest factories are sub-contractors producing high-volume, low-cost garments for the North American and western European markets. A rapidly developing source of sub-contracted production is eastern Europe, North Africa and Turkey, where the factories generally work on shorter runs and at higher levels of technology than their counterparts who are based further away from their markets.

Working methods (Fig. 1.2)

The manufacturer can produce garments via a sub-contractor in a number of ways, for example:

(1) *Cutting* The manufacturer can supply the sub-contractor with:
   • cut garments ready for sewing;
   • raw materials and cutting markers;
   • raw materials and graded sets of patterns.
(2) *Making-up* This is the raison-d'etre of the sub-contractor and is the basic service he sells.
(3) *Trimmings* The manufacturer can supply all, some or none of the trimmings required to make the garments.
(4) *Finishing* This usually refers to pressing, final inspection and bagging, and one or more of these processes can be performed by the manufacturer or the sub-contractor.
(5) *Quality control* The manufacturer usually operates in-process and final quality control procedures to ensure that the garments produced by the sub-contractor are according to specifications.

A general term to encompass all of these aspects is cut, make and trim (CMT) and a sub-contractor will often be referred to as a CMT operation.

Sourcing company

The sourcing company takes the sub-contractor definition a step further within the context of global sourcing. Using the UK clothing industry as an example (which has been mirrored throughout economically developed countries), we have witnessed the mutation of large-scale clothing manufacturers from 'manufacturers on own account' to 'sourcing companies' via the increased reliance upon globally dispersed 'sub-contractors'. This latest incarnation of the clothing manufacturer is

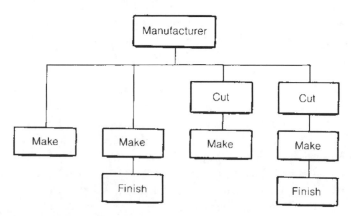

Fig. 1.2 Manufacturer and sub-contractors

typified by the proximity of the sourcing company to the retailer (and hence the eventual consumer market for the product) and its distance from the manufacturer – and with this change in association a new relationship has evolved between the functions. An emerging structure links retailers directly with what were once sub-contactors managed by sourcing companies, thus raising the status of the sub-contractor to that of manufacturer on own account. Yet it is fair to say that the sourcing company plays a vital role in bridging the gap between manufacturer and retailer. Functions such as design, pattern engineering and product development are best held close to the market, and preferably for the retailer not as one of their overheads.

To sum up

Although they are running different types of businesses, the manufacturer, the sub-contractor and the sourcing company need similar management skills in order to meet the challenges facing them from day to day. They need the ability to plan and control production, and in some instances to supervise labour, to achieve high productivity and ensure appropriate quality levels.

2 Sectors of the Clothing Industry

Introduction

The scope of the clothing industry has been defined as 'the manufacture of garments worn on the body, and this excludes the extremities, e.g. hats, gloves, stockings, socks and shoes'. According to this definition, the main sectors of the industry are:

- waterproof outerwear;
- men's tailored outerwear;
- women's tailored outerwear;
- casual clothing and sportswear;
- shirts;
- blouses;
- dresses;
- underwear;
- foundation garments;
- lingerie and pyjamas;
- children's wear (also sub-divided according to garment types);
- work clothes and uniforms;
- knitwear (adults and children's).

Most of these sectors can be divided into sub-sectors, depending on the degrees of specialisation required and/or the scale of production. For example, in a sector such as waterproof outerwear, some factories could produce rainwear for men, women and children while others could specialise in just one of these products. While it is true that manufacturers in one particular sector will generally try to expand horizontally in order to cover the market for their basic product as widely as possible, it has become increasingly necessary for them build in the flexibility to cope with diverse product changes.

There are some overlaps between the sectors as regards technologically related products. A typical example is between men's shirts and ladies' tailored blouses, where there are close similarities in the basic process and production technologies used. Some of the semi-automatic machines which could be used interchangeably for men's shirts and women's tailored blouses are collar profile stitchers, cuff sewers and pocket setters. Sequential buttonholers and button sewers are another example of common process technologies for shirts and blouses. Commonalities like these can help minimise the frequent underutilisation of semi-automated manufacturing technologies.

What were once marginal producers creating 'pop' fashions for young men and women have, with the increased importance of 'fast fashion', been transformed into a major section of the industry. These are usually smaller factories and they turn their hands to whatever the market demands at any particular moment. The production runs in these factories are very short, with radically different garments being produced one after the other or sometimes simultaneously. These types of producers are the true entrepreneurs of the clothing industry. They have to guess right and encapsulate the entire process of producing garments into two or three weeks or less, as against the four to six months which most large-scale manufacturers normally require.

The overall trend is for the demarcation lines between the sectors to become more marked as a result of the global shift in clothing manufacture. The need for reduced lead times in the 'fast fashion' sector is diametrically opposed to the requirements of less rapidly changing products. Thus, proximity to market becomes an important aspect of the smaller, more versatile producer.

Garment types

Another important and more practical classification of the garments produced by the clothing industry is based on two parameters:

(1) *Style variation*   The extent to which the design, fabric and make-up of the basic garment produced varies from style to style.
(2) *Frequency*   The rate at which the changes take place, i.e. twice a week or twice a year.

These two factors have a great bearing on the type of organisation and manufacturing facilities required to produce the garments in question. Obviously, if the basic garments remain virtually unchanged for long periods of time, the production lines can be highly engineered and standardised. On the other hand, drastic style variations occurring at frequent intervals require a quick-response organisation and production system which provides the maximum flexibility and adaptability.

Using these two parameters, most garments can be classified under four headings (Fig. 2.1).

(1) *Staple product*   This type of garment has almost continuous production and, apart from occasional minor changes in cloth, colour and cut, remains

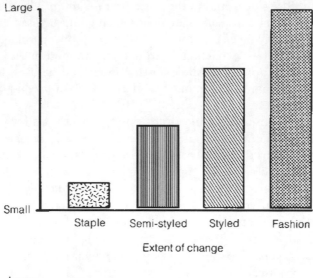

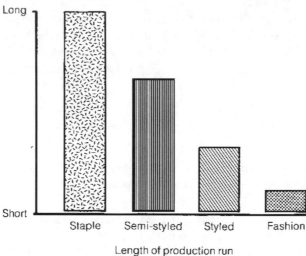

Fig. 2.1   Product types – the factors of change and production runs

basically unchanged from year to year. Two typical examples of staple products are men's underwear and industrial work clothes, such as overalls or warehouse coats.

(2) *Semi-styled product*   A basic type of garment but with minor variations from style to style. The cloth and colours change quite frequently and the production runs per cloth and style are considerably shorter than those for staple products. Men's classic shirts are an example of a semi-styled product where slight variations could include changes in the cloth colour and pattern, collar shape, type of pockets, sleeve lengths and cuff shapes.

(3) *Styled product*   This is based on one type of garment but with substantial and frequent styling changes. The cloth and colours change from style to style

and the product runs are somewhat shorter than for semi-styled products. Ladies' skirts, jackets, dresses and coats are typical examples of styled products.

(4) *Fashion product*   This is the type of garment that has extreme and abrupt changes in design and cloth from one style to another. Production runs are very short and time is of the essence in order to exploit sudden, short-term demands.

In some respects the fashion product sector can be likened to a research and development operation for the clothing industry. The more successful and lasting fashions generated by this sector will attract the attention of a larger group of consumers who want to be 'in fashion' but are prepared to wait and want to pay less for the privilege. So the more durable fashions pass on to the mass-production sectors and the garments reach the general public at popular prices after a delay of a few months to a year. A classic example of a durable fashion is the famous Coco Chanel suit, which was first introduced during the early 1950s and at that time was considered the peak of haute couture fashion. With minor changes, this style remained popular for many years and was mass produced many times during its long history.

Although there are basic demarcation lines between product groups, this does not mean that a specific garment type can only belong to one group. A case in point is a man's shirt which, depending on the extent of the fashion element in its design and fabric, can be produced in each of the four product groups. The same applies to many other types of garment.

To sum up

The crux of the matter is not whether a garment is a staple or a fast-fashion product but rather the type of organisation and facilities required to produce it efficiently and profitably.

3 Product Types and Organisation

Each of the four product types examined in the previous chapter requires a particular combination of organisation and production capabilities for its manufacture. The essential difference between each combination is based on time.

A company having a relatively long-term production programme for a few similar products requires a totally different organisational and operational set-up to that of a manufacturer producing a large variety of styles in very small batches.

More time allows long-term planning and development and the application of sophisticated techniques at all levels. Other than in exceptional circumstances, decisions are considered rather than instinctive, and reactive responses can be finely calculated.

Less time creates an environment where immediate decisions and instant reactions are the order of the day. In this situation success or failure depends on the collective ability of the company to improvise and adapt quickly to changing circumstances.

Time influences every function in the company and so determines its organisational and operational structure. Some of the other important factors which have a direct bearing on this structure are:

- unit size;
- production run duration;
- operator skills;
- salary levels;
- engineering;
- marketing and design.

Unit size

This refers to the physical size of a production unit, which could be an entire factory or one of a number of small units within a factory. In the main, small factories operate as one unit, while it is common for large factories to be organised with central cutting and finishing departments etc., which serve a number of production units. These sub-units can all be under one roof or spread over a number of locations and could possibly include sub-contractors.

There are many determinants of unit size, but in operative terms management would plan for the optimum combination of manpower and equipment that is commensurate with the type of garment to be produced and the targeted output level for the unit.

A limiting factor on the size of a unit could be an expensive semi-automatic machine that performs a standard operation: the average daily output of the machine would dictate the staffing level and the equipment of the unit it supplies. There are always exceptional circumstances where management would knowingly be prepared to underutilise expensive equipment for reasons of output requirements or as a 'safety-first' precaution in case of lengthy breakdowns.

For example, if the output required from the unit is more than the capacity of one type of special machine but less than that of two machines, a small loss from the underutilization of the second machine would be acceptable when measured against the greater benefits of increased total production from the manufacturing unit.

While the domination of large single pieces of semi-automated machinery has arguably diminished in line with changes in market demand for staple products, there still exist many examples of how the unit size of various departments in a clothing factory is determined by the capacities of specific machinery and equipment. Overall, the aim of management is to find the most balanced combination possible within, and between, all the units which together make a factory.

Production run duration

This is the period of time for which one garment type is produced by one unit and, depending on the product type, this time could be measured in months, weeks or days. The length of the production run affects many aspects of the production structure, one of the most important being the size of the production unit.

It is well known in the clothing industry that the introduction of a new style into production requires a running-in learning period before the unit reaches optimum output levels. The length of the running-in period depends on two factors: the change in fabric and/or the number of new operations which have to be learned by the operators on the line. Examples are given here of these two factors.

Change in fabric

The simplest example would be that of a factory running one style in two different fabrics, 100% wool and 100% polyester. If the unit had been working for some time on the woollen cloth and then had to switch over to the synthetic, the operators would require some time to adapt to the very different sewing and handling characteristics of the polyester cloth, and the engineers and technicians would require time to adjust/change the machinery in order to cope with the change in fabric type. The amount of time the unit required to reach peak production would obviously vary according to the unit's total experience in switching over to different types of fabrics. In any event, some production would be lost until the unit as a whole reached a balanced and optimum standard of output.

New operations

The number of operations to be learned every time a new style is introduced would depend on the product type manufactured by the company. In a staple product environment, the changeover to a new style could possibly involve the learning of one or two different operations, while style changes in fashion products could require a substantial number of new operations to be learned and mastered. In both cases, the time needed would depend on the versatility and adaptability of the operators.

The learning time for a new style is governed by the proportion of each of the following operations in the production: standard operations, transfer operations and new operations.

Standard operations

Where a unit is producing garments with the same basic component structure, such as ladies' trousers, many of the operations are common to nearly every style produced. Changes in fabric might require a short time for the operator to become acclimatised to working on a different cloth, but the overall learning time for the unit would be minimal.

Transfer operations

This would apply where the operators have all the basic skills and experience required to perform the operations, but need to adapt them to different applications. An example of a transfer operation is where an operator is employed on top-stitching the edges of garments. The results of style changes could mean that the operator has to adapt to different shapes of collars, lapels and fronts in addition to possible variations in threads and top-stitch widths. The operator does not have to learn a new operation from scratch, but rather has to apply existing expertise to very similar situations. While some time would be required for the operator to 'get the hang of' a new style, this would be relatively short.

New operations

This means exactly what it says: the operator has all the basic skills and experience but must learn completely new operations. This situation frequently arises in the manufacture of styled and fashion merchandise and, depending on the complexity of the new operations, the time required to build up pace and quality can be quite considerable.

The final number of standard, transfer and new operations required for a new style, when combined with the size of the average production order given to the unit, can also have a very considerable effect on unit size.

It is an established fact that the longer operators work on one style, the more their efficiency improves, and more opportunities exist for engineering these operations, until productivity reaches very high levels. When this has occurred, the operation is at its most viable for both management and staff. Therefore when establishing the composition of a production unit, it is in everyone's interest that the unit should be able to work on one style for as long as possible. In practical terms this involves some simple arithmetic, and the following example illustrates the principles. The calculations are based on the following conditions:

Direct production staff	120 operators
Working day	8 hours net
Average size of production order	1200 units
Average work content of typical garment	1.25 hours

The formula used to calculate the duration of the product run for units of various sizes is:

$$\frac{\text{Average production order size} \times \text{Work content of typical garment}}{\text{Number of operators} \times \text{Net hours worked per day per operator}}$$

Accordingly, if the unit were given an average production order quantity of a typical garment, the length of the production run would be:

$$\frac{1200 \text{ units} \times 1.25 \text{ hours}}{120 \text{ operators} \times 8 \text{ hours}} = 1.56 \text{ days}$$

Extending this calculation to units of other sizes, the results would be:

Unit size	Production run
60 operators	3.13 days
40 operators	4.69 days
30 operators	6.25 days

So all things being equal, the factory management would attempt to build small production units and give them relatively long production runs of one style, rather than use large units which would never have sufficient time to reach the same output levels – in this sense, 'small is good'.

Operator skills

This is another subject which influences the operational structure of a factory because operator training time and flexibility have an important effect on production.

Operator skills are concerned with the number of operations an operator can perform proficiently, and how much training time is needed to bring the operator up to the requisite standards of output and quality. An example of skills grading for sewing operations is:

(1) *Unskilled* Able to perform one or two simple, low-skill operations only, such as thread-cleaning or bar-tacking buttonholes. Training time would be measured in days.
(2) *Semi-skilled* Knows all the operations required to sew simple assemblies, e.g. joining backs and fronts, assembling body linings or setting them into the garment. The cumulative training time could be several weeks.
(3) *Skilled* Can carry out complex and critical operations, like sleeve and collar setting or the assembly of intricate components. An operator at this level would require three or four months of training, including time spent on the line, before achieving the necessary standards.
(4) *Highly skilled* This is an increasingly rare species of operator who is capable of sewing a complete garment and can adapt very quickly to style changes. It would take a long period of training and experience for an operator to reach this level.

The ratio of supervisors to operators is also a function of operator skill levels as it is generally recognised that lower-skilled operators require closer supervision than the more skilled and experienced workers.

Salary levels

The salaries paid in each factory can be a result of prevailing local supply and demand, but in the main salary structure is directly linked to the operator skill levels required by the factory. A large factory manufacturing staple products which can be broken down into a number of simple and easily learned operations would have an operator salary structure on, or very close to, the lowest permissible level. On the other hand, operators working at the top end of the 'instant' fashion scale would demand and receive far greater salaries then their unskilled or semi-skilled counterparts in other factories.

With the increasingly globalised nature of the clothing manufacturing industry, salary levels vary greatly from one country to another (Table 1.5). This, combined with proximity to market, has encouraged the fragmentation of the industry.

Engineering

One of the preconditions for using sophisticated production engineering techniques is the continuity and stability of the basic product manufactured in the factory. Where the product range has a large number of operations common to most of the styles produced, these operations can be engineered by specialised

semi-automatic or computerised machinery and equipment. As a rule, small repetitive operations lend themselves best to engineering, and this is exploited to the
full by the staple product type of factory. Because of the lengths of their production runs, these factories also invest in special, purpose-built fixtures and attachments for the non-standard operations in new styles.

The smaller and more versatile factories would normally hesitate to invest large
sums of money in specialised machinery capable of one or two operations only.
This type of factory is equipped with basic types of machinery and attachments
and relies more on the skills of its operators than on high-tech equipment.

Considerable differences in the types of incentive schemes used to encourage and
motivate operator output can also be found in the various types of factories. The
line engineering staff of a staple product factory would have the time and techniques available to analyse work content in fine detail, using conventional or computerised methods. Consequently the time standards issued to operators would be
very accurate and capable of rapid updating. A factory working on short production runs of a large variety of products would, in the time available, be hard pressed
to establish accurate standards for the production of each style. If this type of
factory has a payment by results system, the time standards would be based more
on historical data and 'guestimates' than on production engineering procedures.

In this type of production unit, production engineering plays a very small role,
if any, and output levels are achieved and maintained more through dynamic management than through incentive schemes.

Marketing and design

Large organisations producing staple garments usually work hand in hand with
big retailers, and most factories of this type dedicate the bulk of their production
to one or two customers only. This situation greatly simplifies the processes of
design, sales and distribution.

Fewer designs are needed because staple garments are 'bread and butter' merchandise at the middle to lower end of the fashion scale. Accepted designs generate relatively large orders and can take up the production capacity of the factory
for long periods. In addition, as there are only one or two major customers being
served, there is no need for an extensive sales organisation. Distribution is also far
less complicated because the finished garments are delivered either in bulk to the
central warehouses of the retailer or in large batches directly to the shops.

The smaller manufacturer, however, has continually to offer new designs to a
large number of customers so as to obtain sufficient orders to make the production of each style viable. The need for this dynamic and aggressive approach places
extra demands upon the design and product development functions of a manufacturer. These 'knowledge-based' or 'creative' roles require highly skilled indi-
viduals working holistically with the organisation, and each other, as a team.
Indeed, many observers suggest that these 'clever jobs' are the key to keeping some
clothing manufacturing function within industrially developed countries. As most
business is done with smaller retailers, the sales organisation has to be sufficiently

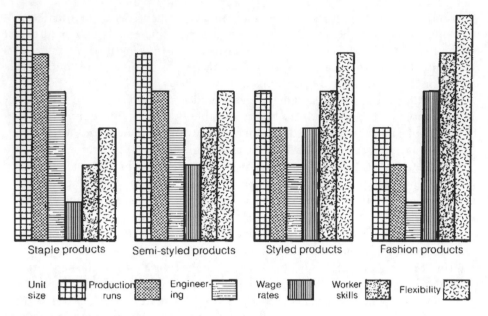

Fig. 3.1 Operational factors according to product types

extensive to cover and service a large number of customers. Warehousing and distribution is also more complex because of the small quantities and large variety of merchandise which has to be delivered to many different customers all over the country.

The relationship between operational factors and product type manufactured is shown in Figure 3.1.

To sum up

This section has shown how the operational structure of a clothing factory is determined, first and foremost, by the product type manufactured. Situations can differ slightly between factories in each product group, but in the final analysis economies of scale have far more relevance for a large factory than for a small one. However, the dominance of larger factories has diminished in industrialised countries and far more importance is placed on the flexibility of the unit than on a highly engineered environment.

Part 2

THE ORGANISATION OF A CLOTHING FACTORY

4 Principles of Management

There are many definitions of management, and a fitting one is:

'The accomplishment of desired objectives by establishing an environment favourable to performance by people operating in organised groups.' (18)

The management function is essential for all organised activity and at all levels of the organisation from the managing director down to a supervisor responsible for a small section within the factory. While the managing director has full executive control and authority for conducting the affairs of the company, the supervisor has similar powers on a far smaller scale. Both of them are managers in the sense that they are organising and regulating the activities of the people within their control.

In order to achieve the specified objectives of the company, management has to perform five basic functions so as to coordinate group activity:

- planning;
- organisation;
- staffing;
- direction;
- control.

All managerial activities can be classified under these headings and their elements are described in the rest of this chapter.

Planning

Planning means deciding in advance how to allocate available and potential resources in order to fulfil the objectives which have been set. These resources can be classified in the following groups:

What?

This concerns the materials required and involves not only cloth, lining and trimmings but also all the other auxiliary materials needed to produce garments, such as chalk, marker papers and pins.

Where?

This is the resource of space. The availability of space must be taken into account when planning the storage of raw materials, or production areas or facilities required, or the warehousing of finished goods.

Who?

This planning element is concerned with human resources: not just production operators, but also the people required to perform all the managerial, supervisory and service functions within the factory.

How?

The question asked here is how will the work be performed? The answer entails evaluating methods, considering the capability of existing machinery and ascertaining whether additional or different machinery is required. This planning element takes into account every section within the factory, and not just the sewing room.

When?

This is the axis of all planning and the timescale dictates which activities have to be performed and when they should be completed. The 'What', 'Where', 'Who' and 'How' elements have to be coordinated along the time axis to ensure that they are available when required. While this remains a very important aspect for those manufacturers producing garment types 1–3 (Chapter 2), because seasons for these products have fixed start and finish dates and accurate timing is necessary in order to exploit fully the trading periods available, fashion product (garment type 4) manufacturers are ruled by a 'now' rather than a 'when' approach.

The coordinated planning of these five elements bridges the gap from where we are to where we want to go. Without planning, events are left to chance and the organisation will be reactive instead of proactive.

Organisation

Organisation is not an end in itself, but rather a means to achieve the required results; there has to be a structure which makes it possible to attain the planned

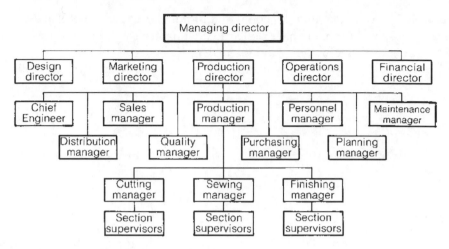

Fig. 4.1 Conventional organisation chart

objectives of the company. Wherever the responsibility of management is vested in more than one person, there must be a pattern of relationships between the various management responsibilities. These patterns involve the delegation of a major responsibility into specialist areas. This division creates an organisation structure and, as most practical managers know, it is organisation which dictates performance.

Organisation structures can be formal or informal, the difference being the degree of demarcation between the functions. In a formal type of organisation the demarcation lines are strictly observed and matters have to go through prescribed hierarchial and bureaucratic procedures. An informal or more 'free-wheeling' type of organisation has overlaps between the various functions which encourage more direct approaches and shorter procedures.

An example of a conventional organisation chart is shown in Figure 4.1. Apart from the longitudinal relationships within the functions, there would also be a framework of lateral relationships between the functions, especially at the higher levels of the organisation.

While the main objective of an organisation chart is to define the management relationships within a company, it is not always necessary to draw up detailed charts. For an organisation to operate effectively, it is far more important that everyone knows their areas of authority and responsibility and coordinates their activities accordingly. An organisation framework is one thing, but it is the operation within it that really counts.

Staffing

This function is basically concerned with people and training, and its short- and long-term objectives are to provide the organisation with the right types and quantities of managerial and non-managerial staff as and when they are needed. All managers perform a staffing function, and although the personnel department of the company will probably have done the preliminary selection and interviewing, the final decision is usually taken by a manager.

Ensuring the correct flow of manpower to a company involves the following factors.

Recruitment

Some of the sources are schools, jobcentres, universities and responses to advertisements.

Selection

There is no magic formula by which a company can ensure that the people it hires will prove wholly suitable for its needs. Depending on the level of the position, there are various physical, psychometric and psychological tests which, if interpreted by an expert, can to a large extent eliminate some of the risks involved when engaging new staff.

Training

Systematic selection helps in obtaining the best labour available, but these efforts can be wasted if the new employees are not well inducted and correctly trained. This applies to all levels because even a new manager requires some degree of training by his superiors.

Direction

The function of direction is concerned with getting employees to accomplish their set tasks effectively. Planning, organising and staffing alone will not get the job done, any more than starting the engine of a car will make it move. It is the function of direction which breathes life into planning and organisation: plans do not achieve themselves.

The behaviour of a group largely depends on the type of manager it has, and good managers will always provide their subordinates with the information necessary for intelligent action. Obviously, the more a person knows about his or her own work and environment, the more intelligently they can work.

Control

The managerial function of control is the measurement and correction of performance in order to ensure that the company's objectives are accomplished as planned. This function involves three steps:

(1) establishment of standards;
(2) measurement of performance;
(3) correction of deviations.

Establishment of standards

Standards are criteria against which actual results can be measured. They can be physical and represent quantities of products or materials, or they can be stated in monetary terms, such as costs and income. All the established standards are used as the basis for the second step.

Measurement of performance

This involves the comparison of actual results with those planned. Three of the most important comparative measurements of production are those of costs, output and quality.

Costs

Budgets are prepared for all the cost centres in the company and, apart from raw materials, the largest single item where cost is incurred is the production department as a whole, not just direct labour. A periodic report on the financial performance of this department would show the results for the period and the position of the total budget to date. The example in Table 4.1 shows these comparative measurements where the current period is one month (period 2) within a three-month budget. The to-date figures show the performance since this budget was introduced: the budget has been in operation for two months (periods 1 and 2) and the cumulative loss is £150.

Table 4.1 Example of production department costs

Item	Period 2			Periods 1 and 2	
	Budget	Actual	Variance	Budget	Variance
Wages	5000	5100	−100	10250	−160
Social premiums	1250	1275	−25	2560	−40
Rent	150	150	—	300	—
Rates	75	75	—	150	—
Power and lighting	200	180	+20	420	+10
Air conditioning	60	50	+10	125	—
Machine spares	250	190	+60	500	+40
General maintenance	100	120	−20	200	−10
Canteen	250	260	−10	510	—
Cleaning	80	80	—	160	—
Divers	50	40	+10	100	+10
Total	7465	7520	(55)	15275	−150

Table 4.2 Production value report

Style No.	Quantity	Making-up price	Total value
6722	310	5.0	1550
6724	260	4.8	1248
6112	120	2.9	348
6113	160	2.9	464
6428	280	3.0	840
6437	370	3.1	1147
Total production value for period			5597
Actual costs for period			5150
Variance			+447

Table 4.3 Quality report

Item	Period 5	Periods 1 to 4
Total produced	1450	5945
Total rejected	29	107
Reject rate	2%	1.8%
Standard reject rate	1.6%	1.6%
Variance	−0.4%	−0.2%
% reject rate: standard rate	+25%	+12½%

Output

This can be measured in terms of monetary value or units. A very accurate picture is obtained from a control system based on production value, which is the total number of garments produced in a given period multiplied by their costed, making-up prices. The total production value is then compared to the actual costs for the same period, as shown in Table 4.2.

Quality

It is realistic to assume that, however well the quality control procedures operate within a factory, there will always be a certain percentage of garments rejected for one reason or another. The majority of factories know their quality performance levels by experience and/or by comparison with other companies producing similar merchandise, and each factory will establish a standard as a criterion for measuring quality achievements. A simple example of a control report on quality is shown in Table 4.3; in practice the report would be far more detailed, giving the causes of rejection and highlighting trends.

Correction of deviations

When organised planning and control procedures are operated, it is relatively easy to expose deviations and to apply corrective measures. In the main, the efficacy and promptness of these measures is directly related to the accuracy and extent of the control procedures in use.

Feedback is central to the correction of deviations; this informational input provides the basis for all operational decisions regarding the non-achievement of plans. A large factory would probably have control and feedback systems which would report on production every hour throughout the day. If minus deviations are discovered after, say, two hours' work, then at least management has a better chance of correcting them early on than if the deviations are reported only at the end of the day when it is too late to do anything about them. Every working day brings its own problems, and today's failures are very difficult to correct tomorrow.

The feedback principle involves a closed circle (Fig. 4.2) which has the following main elements:

(1) *Planning* This produces the long- and short-term production programmes.
(2) *Performance* The control function measures the production results and compares them to the plan.
(3) *Feedback* This is the process whereby the deviations exposed by the control function are reported back to management.
(4) *Re-planning* The information supplied by the feedback loop is used to re-plan the production programme as and when necessary.
(5) *Objectives* All the previous elements are directed towards achieving the planned aims.

While most feedback systems provide real-time information, this in itself is not sufficient to run a factory efficiently. Ideally a control system should detect possi-

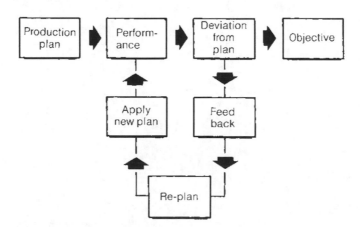

Fig. 4.2 The feedback ring

ble deviations before they actually occur, by forecasting via simulations what is likely to happen tomorrow or the day after. Although this type of reporting might contain a small margin of error, it is better than having a detailed report on yesterday's output figures, about which the production manager can do little or nothing.

To sum up

The principles of management are the same for every clothing factory – or indeed any factory – the only difference being that of scale. While the basic purposes of factories may vary, all of them rely on the effectiveness of management in all functions for the attainment of their objectives.

5 Design Department

Introduction

Until the early 1960s, the world fashion scene was dominated by a long list of French designers such as Dior, Givenchy, Balmain and Balenciaga. While most of their designs were directed towards the moneyed classes, it is fair to say that during the period of their domination most of the mass-produced fashion merchandise on the market owed its origins to their designs.

Today there are a great number of high profile 'named' designers on the international fashion scene and this provides the average consumer with a very wide choice of fresh and original designs, instead of slightly dated, watered-down versions of the work of a relatively few couturiers. Designers such as Muir, Valentino, Kenzo, Lagerfeld and Blass, although having a salon clientele, are also orientated towards the popular market and their clothes are mass-produced and sold all over the world. This level of consumer choice, coupled with complex global supply networks, is the key feature that defines the clothing industry of today.

It is beyond the scope of this book to examine the workings of the world of fashion in great detail, but an excellent picture is given by Nicholas Coleridge in his book *The Fashion Conspiracy* (7). This section will examine the organisation and activities of the design department in relation to the product type manufactured by the factory.

The design department can be considered as the research and development department of a clothing factory, because it is in this department that the prototypes of garments are developed and prepared for selling and production. For most factories the process of product development involves seven stages:

(1) forecasting;
(2) designing;
(3) collection planning;
(4) pattern making;
(5) technology;

(6)   production of sample garments;
(7)   pattern grading.

Stages 1–3 are most likely to take place 'close to market' whereas stages 4–7 are likely to occur 'close to production', reflecting the globally dispersed nature of the industry.

Forecasting

This stage commences with the evaluation and interpretation of the market's future needs in terms of fashion and price. Apart from intuition and common sense, these forecasts are based on the accumulated knowledge, expertise and experience of the company to make a fairly accurate prediction of the types of garments customers will buy and the prices they will be willing to pay.

When considering the market for a clothing manufacturer's products, it is important to appreciate that the manufacturer is concerned with the needs of the final consumer and the needs of the intermediary retailer. Clearly an open and communicative relationship is necessary; retailers and manufacturers that have worked together for many years develop a symbiotic existence.

Fashion trends

For the general public, the main fashion forecasts come from the fashion shows held in New York, Paris, Milan and London and the publicity given to such shows by the media. These collections are important to the global fashion styling trends but are inaccessible to most consumers.

With regard to clothing design, there are the creators of trends and there are the followers of trends. Other than the big name designers, most designers have to rely on the fashion grapevine and the trade shows for advance indications of what are likely to be the main trends for the coming season. Today, mass media channels are increasingly providing rapid access to emerging trends and styles. TV, Web and printed information featuring celebrities (at all status levels, and for all kinds of reasons) exhibiting elite designs inspire mass market designers and consumers alike. Yet it is arguable that both elite designers and mass market designers have access to, and are increasingly influenced by, other fashion systems such as street style, sport, music and ethnic culture rather than the catwalk shows themselves.

Part of the grapevine are cloth merchants or mills who, because they have to prepare fabrics so far in advance, will have a pretty accurate idea of what is being sampled by the big houses. This is an interesting aspect of the 'fast fashion' revolution. While clothing assembly lead times have been reduced considerably, fewer strategies exist for the compression of production times for woven or knitted textiles; arguably, the trends for fabric colour and texture are dictated well in advance by the fabric producers and their own interaction with designers. Today there is also a very large international trade in textiles and consequently there is a cross fertilisation of ideas and gossip.

Another little-known source of advance information are the fashion trade shows. These trade shows are held well in advance of the seasonal shows and the garments displayed are designed by what are, in effect, fashion forecasters. Mainly based in Paris, these houses try to present the styling, fabrics and colours which they forecast will be in the name designers' collections. Their knowledge is gleaned from all kinds of sources connected with the leading houses and this, together with their own ability as designers, enables them to present collections containing fairly reliable forecasts.

The shows held by these forecasters have very high admission charges and the customer is able to buy toile copies of the designs with samples of the cloth and trim. These viewings are usually very well attended by people from the clothing industry, and so it should be no surprise that at the beginning of a new season the majority of retailers show the same basic designs in the same range of cloths and colours.

For companies producing 'instant' fashion, the big fashion shows are a very important source of design input. As these companies work close to the start of the season and are organised for quick response, they can go to the market with closer versions of the main fashion features than most other manufacturers.

Apart from viewing various types of fashion shows, most designers will also attend one or more of the textile exhibitions held periodically throughout the world. These exhibitions are an important part of design input because fabrics, colours and textures can also inspire design ideas. In addition to these shows, prediction companies such as Promostyl and Design Intelligence produce glossy forecasting manuals that forecast a range of trends for the fashion industry each season covering yarns, knits, colours, fabrics, and styling and accessories, which can be purchased by fashion and clothing companies. Prediction companies gather global information from diverse sources such as world events, music, cinema, art and culture, ethnic and street, and designer collections, and interpret this information to predict trends about two years in advance. Such prediction companies also offer a service that involves presenting the season's trends directly to groups of designers. Many fashion and clothing companies subscribe to Internet-based prediction companies like Worth Global Style Network (WGSN), which is now a key trend research tool for many mass market designers. The Internet in general is also a key source for market research and ideas.

The information gathered at fashion and textile shows and from other sources has to be interpreted by the designer to establish the best mix for the particular category of customers served by the company. For example, a house producing expensive merchandise would present the forecasted styles with little or no changes from those exhibited at the trade shows. Against that, a manufacturer producing for mass markets would show watered-down versions of the same styles using cheaper materials and a simpler make-up.

Irrespective of how the designs for a collection are arrived at, each company has the same objective: that the projected new styles must be commercially viable in the sense that they will motivate the public to buy new clothes, especially those produced by the company. Although the objective is to produce a different range each season, there is an overlap from one season to another. A range will actually include best-sellers from the previous season in new colours, fabrics and trims, fashion predicted for that season, and new styles introduced to test the market. Great care is taken to ensure a smooth transition from one season to another rather than breaking new ground each season.

The designer has a key role in a clothing company and is responsible for the implementation of a design policy which takes into account the company's resources, customers and marketing objectives. Because of the nature of the clothing industry, the designer must accurately project these objectives at least one season ahead and produce garments which incorporate the total aims of the company.

Price structure

The clothing industry works to a price structure based on the different price and fashion sectors of the clothing market. For men's, women's and children's clothing it is generally accepted that there are five consumer groups (Fig. 5.1), where group A represents the expensive, high-fashion end and group E the cheapest sector of the market. Group C is the largest section of the market and purchases popularly priced, mass-produced, durable merchandise.

This price structure dictates the prices which clothing producers can obtain for a specific range of products. The manufacturer must produce garments at a price which, when the regular retail gross profit margin is added, gives an acceptable selling price for that particular sector of the market. Consequently a forecast has to be made of the ex-factory prices which will be acceptable to the company's customers, and this involves estimating what can be invested in an average garment as regards labour and materials, and trying to find the optimum combination of these. A forecast of this type also tries to take into account the economic trends at home and abroad, currency rates, export subsidies, etc. and if possible a 'guestimate' of what the competition is planning to do.

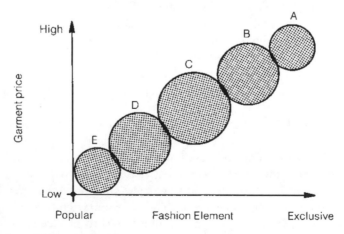

Fig. 5.1   Market sectors

Working from rough design ideas, the designer and the marketing people together invest a lot of thought and effort in honing the two forecasts of design trends and price structure so as to hit the projected targets most effectively. These two forecasts provide the input for the next stage, which is designing the garments that will form the core of the collection for the next season.

Designing

In practice, the designer starts by preparing some sketches of the core ideas for the collection and selecting the fabrics and trim to be used for each design. These core designs are garments which contain the main design and fabric features of the collection and they will be used as the themes for developing the full range of samples. For example, four or five core designs might represent the basic ideas of the collection and each one of these could lead to several variations.

The designs themselves can be hand-drawn and coloured, or produced using a computerised design system such as 2-D CAD. These systems are an important tool in the design process today for most clothing businesses, primarily as a communication tool to speed up the design cycle and connect with other members of the design team. For many companies CAD provides an unambiguous format in which to communicate design details and specifications with the offshore production units.

Working on a computerised system, the designer can start either by sketching the rough outlines of the design with a stylus on the tablet in front of the screen (Fig. 5.2), or by calling up a similar form which was used previously for another style. The silhouette and interior style lines can be easily modified, and the system retains the exact proportions of the design while the changes are being made. During this process, the screen display can be rotated and angled so that the designer has a three-dimensional picture of the design throughout each stage of its development.

The finished design can be coloured by a number of different methods, which include:

(1) For plain cloths, the designer merely selects a colour from the series of palettes displayed on the screen and the line drawing is coloured automatically. The colour itself can be darkened or lightened so as to achieve the exact shade desired. In addition, the coloured display can be illuminated at different angles and intensities of lighting so as to simulate the internal and display lighting of retail stores.

(2) These computerised systems also have a textile design option whereby a fabric can be designed directly on the screen. A grid and measurement feature maintains design and pattern repeat proportions, and when the design is finalised it can be coloured in any combination of colours and be given a textural appearance such as tweedy, high-pile or satiny. The completed cloth design is then applied to the outline drawing and the designer has a complete

picture of the projected garment and cloth combination. Some of the more sophsticated systems have an option to give cloths a draping factor, such as stiff, pliable or soft, and this can be applied to the design to enhance the total picture of the garment. Modifications can easily be made to the garment and fabric designs until the most preferable combination is achieved.

(3)   Where the designer is working from a collection of previously selected fabrics, a simple method of photography is used to record them. A section of each of the sample cloths is scanned by a video camera, which records the design, colour and texture of the cloth and then transfers this information to the computer. The designer can then call up the garment design and apply the selected cloth to it. Where a cloth has been chosen in different colours, these are displayed at the side of the screen and the designer can try out the possible variations.

The garment design layouts for the core collection, whether hand- or computer-drawn, are now ready to be used for the next stage of the sampling process: collection planning.

Collection planning

This process is, in effect, the pre-production phase of sampling, and the objectives are to set out in detail the styles, fabrics and colours which will represent the

Fig. 5.2   Computerised design system by Lectra cutting systems

company's proposals for the forthcoming season. The designer works in close cooperation with the marketing department and together they attempt to determine the best possible style, fabric and price combinations for the company's customers. For maximum production efficiency the designer (or technical designer) should work closely with the assembly function of the business at this stage. The earlier consideration can be given to assembly techniques/requirements (without compromising the integrity of the design), the fewer problems will be encountered during production. It is a widely held belief that 75% of costs are dictated by decisions made at the design stage, yet they occur in, and are inappropriately attributed to, the manufacturing stage.

Using the sketches of the core collection as a starting point, various alternatives and approaches will be examined, including:

- developing the variations from the core designs;
- trying the same cloth on a number of different designs;
- modifying some of the ideas to make the garments more acceptable to a wider range of customers;
- the addition of 'fill-in' type garments for which, in the opinion of the sales manager, there is always a small but steady demand throughout the season;
- the inclusion of garments which some of the larger buyers have indicated an interest in seeing;
- balancing the contents of the collection so that it contains the optimum style and price combinations for each of the garment categories to be presented.

An example of part of a collection plan for a skirt manufacturer is shown in Figure 5.3 and most well-organised companies produce a similar type of plan. After approval by those concerned, the finalised plan becomes operative and the actual production of samples begins.

Pattern making

This function connects design to production by producing paper templates for all the components, such as cloth, lining and fusibles, which have to be cut for a garment. Pattern making is a highly skilled technique which calls for technical ability, a sensitivity for design interpretation and a practical understanding of the process technology used by the factory. Industrial pattern making has two basic stages, the block pattern and the garment pattern.

The block pattern

This is a basic pattern without any style features and incorporates the measurements, proportions and posture of the body for which garments developed from this pattern are intended. The block pattern can be created by either of the following methods:

- *Flat method*   The components of the pattern, usually the body and sleeve, are constructed by a draft (technical drawing) which incorporates the measurements and proportions of the particular system used by the pattern maker. This type of pattern draft can also be produced by a computer which has been programmed to construct basic patterns according to given measurements and proportions.
- *Modelling*   This was the original method of constructing garment patterns before the advent of flat systems and it is still widely used at the haute couture end of the clothing business. Modelling entails the fitting of the block garment, usually in toile, on a workroom stand of the appropriate size. When the fit and balance are satisfactory, the toile is removed from the stand and each component is copied on to pattern paper and the necessary making-up allowances added.

Flat systems owe their origins to modelling because a pattern draft is only a quick and standardised method of reproducing the basic components which were originally arrived at through modelling.

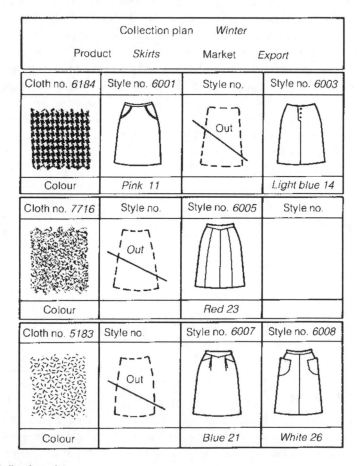

Fig. 5.3   Collection plan

The garment pattern

The styled patterns used for cutting the original sample garments can be developed by a variety of means, including the flat method, modelling or a combination of both. When using the flat method, the pattern maker superimposes the style lines of the garment on to a copy of the block pattern, performs the necessary manipulations and then adds the requisite sewing and other allowances to each component. Related components are aligned to check their accuracy and nips and/or notches are made in the seam lines as guides for alignment and matching during sewing and making-up.

The conventional methods of pattern construction are gradually being replaced by computerised systems which interact with the pattern maker. The essential features of this technology are pattern design and pattern generation systems.

Pattern design systems (PDS)

The pattern maker inputs to the system all the block patterns in current use and with the aid of the computer can construct garment patterns from them. Alternatively, a previously constructed pattern stored in the system can be used as the base pattern for a new style. It is also possible to store specific features such as collars, lapels and pockets; then, providing the pattern maker has inputted matching alignment points, an existing lapel can, for example, be literally 'stuck on' to a different forepart with a minimum of time and effort.

The finalised patterns can be plotted for verification before cutting out, or they can be cut out on a regular plotter using a cutting head instead of a pen. Because of the many set routines built into pattern design systems, the productivity of the pattern maker is substantially higher than can be achieved when using the traditional methods of tracing, drawing, cutting out and marking by hand. The increased productivity of PDS makes a significant reduction in the throughput time of new samples, and this is one of the important factors of quick response technology.

Pattern generation systems (PGS)

When the pattern components for the top cloth have been developed on the computer via PDS, the pattern generation programme automatically generates the patterns for auxiliary components such as linings and fusibles. It operates according to rules specified in advance by the pattern maker on the relationship between top cloth and lining or top cloth and fusibles. The planning matrix of the system can also take into account the characteristics of the top cloth to be used, incorporating this information when generating the auxiliary patterns. A typical example of this is the generation of a top collar from the under collar pattern where, if a heavy cloth is to be used, the fullness allowance would be different from that required for a lightweight fabric.

Technology

Irrespective of the techniques and methods used to construct and perfect the patterns, an important factor which must be taken into account at this stage is the technological capability of the factory and what it can or cannot produce. It is possible that a new style feature requires the use of a special type of machine which the factory does not possess, and this is the time when decisions have to be made as to whether this particular item of equipment should be purchased, or whether an acceptable substitute can be found from what is available in the factory, or whether minor modifications to the design/pattern will allow existing machinery to be utilised.

These technological considerations will apply not only to sewing but also to other manufacturing processes. New types of materials could require a range of fusing conditions which cannot be achieved on the existing equipment. It is also possible that the factory is not equipped to press large quantities of a critical material, when this material is likely to be the predominant cloth for the next season.

All these and many other technological factors have to be considered when sampling. Investment in new machinery and equipment may be justified not by a conventional pay-back calculation, but by a far more pragmatic criterion. The question is not how much money will be 'lost' by purchasing the equipment, but rather how much essential business might be lost if the equipment is not purchased.

Production of sample garments

Sample garments are usually produced by a small unit supervised by the pattern maker and/or the designer, and this unit has an important role in determining the results of the forthcoming season. Separation of the design function from the manufacturing function brings pressure to bear on this phase: can a design department based in one country interact with sample function based in another to fully understand the implications of producing a new range of garments?

Sampling is a continual process in the clothing industry. During the development of new products the following elements arise:

(1) New materials and processes have to be experimented with to establish their suitability for mass production.
(2) The production garment patterns have to be altered and perfected to rectify faults discovered during the making-up of the samples.
(3) At the sampling stage, the quantities of fabric and trimmings are established and a quick costing made. Sometimes the designer and pattern maker will decide to alter a pattern to reduce the amount of material and/or labour required, if the projected cost of the original design exceeds the forecast price.
(4) The finished sample garments undergo a thorough scrutiny to evaluate whether they fit in with the overall picture the company wants to present in this particular collection. It is at this stage that sample garments are accepted or rejected.

As each sample is approved, its cost must be accurately calculated in order to deter-mine the selling price (although selling price is becoming more and more deter-mined by what the market will bear) and whether it fits into the planned price framework for that type of garment. The costing sheet or bill of materials of a garment is a very important document because it contains all the data required to plan, produce and control its production. Information for the costing is gathered from many sources within the factory, and the costing itself is prepared by the finance department for management's approval. An example of a garment costing is shown in Figure 7.2. From a sales and production point of view, sampling is probably the most important of the pre-production activities.

Pattern grading

Pattern grading is the process whereby patterns of different sizes are produced from the original master pattern. This process can be performed either manually, or automatically by a computerised system (Fig. 5.4).

Computerised pattern grading is the link between pattern design and generation and the preparatory stages of cutting. The grades produced by the computer can be used in two ways:

Fig. 5.4 Computerised pattern grading

(1) The patterns can be cut out and used to plan cutting markers manually if necessary.
(2) The graded sizes can be stored in the model files of the computer and recalled when cutting markers for that style are to be planned on the system.

Patterns are graded according to size charts which represent the sizes and average measurements of the population group for which the garments are intended. The charts can be supplied by customers or can be those used by the factory. There are many customers who want to see a range of graded garments for the styles they have ordered before giving their approval for bulk cutting. This is a good opportunity for the factory to check the gradings and other factors which could influence the production and quality of the garments.

To sum up

The design department is a key element in the organisation of a company producing fashion merchandise and its operation requires the same management principles as other departments. While fashion is transient and appears to be capricious, the garments themselves are a result of many months' advance planning and meticulous development.

6 Marketing Department

The marketing department carries out three major functions which, depending on the size and organisational structure of the company, may be combined or may be separate entities within the department. These primary functions are:

(1) *Marketing* This is the generic name for all the activities involved in directing the flow of goods from producers to consumers. The marketing function is concerned with defining the characteristics of the company's actual and potential markets and promoting the company's products and image. To a large extent, the marketing manager has a pivotal role in determining the market orientation and product line of the company.

(2) *Merchandising* This is a specific activity which concerns itself with product development, overall production strategy and the delivery of merchandise to customers. Merchandising has not only to adjust rapidly to market variations, but more importantly to anticipate these changes. During a boom season there could be a sudden influx of orders, and the merchandiser would have to allocate production priorities and attempt to wholly or partially satisfy customers who are crying out for merchandise.

(3) *Sales* The primary elements of the sales process are:
    (a) approaching established or potential customers;
    (b) pre-determining their requirements where possible;
    (c) making a sales presentation;
    (d) answering questions and/or settling objections;
    (e) getting the customer to place an order;
    (f) following up after the merchandise has been delivered to check that the customer is satisfied.

Unlike the promotional activities of advertising and other types of publicity, selling relies on personal contact. Thus the major efforts of the sales staff will be directed towards creating opportunities for making oral presentations while showing the company's samples.

Marketing

Regardless of the size of the company and its organisational structure, the marketing function deals with the following subjects either directly or in conjunction with other departments.

Marketing calendar

This calendar provides the operational framework for a season or longer and sets out all the key marketing events for the period involved. The exact timing and sequence of events will be specified, and among the major items which will appear are:

- finalising the collection plan;
- approving the collection;
- preparing the sales forecast budget;
- arranging dates for customer showings at home and abroad;
- arranging for the company to participate in national and international fashion shows;
- holding meetings with sales personnel prior to the showings in order to acquaint them with the new season's collection;
- producing sample ranges for showrooms, representatives and agents;
- deciding on the styles and quantitites of garments to be produced in advance of customers' orders.

In the more progressive companies, the marketing department will prepare and present an informal critique of its past season's results to try and pinpoint the circumstances and reasons that possibly led to marketing successes and failures. This review will be discussed by all concerned and relevant conclusions implemented when planning the next season's marketing calendar.

Product pricing

The price of a garment is the consensus on its value, and at all times a clothing company has to adjust itself to the market price for its products. This price is determined by the total supply of the product offered by all sellers against the total demand for the product by all buyers. For example, if the majority of clothing manufacturers in a particular region have prepared large stocks of materials and garments in anticipation of a long, cold winter and this forecast is realised, these manufacturers will enjoy a profitable season. However, if the season is not as cold and long as forecasted, then there will be more goods available than demand for them. This will force the manufacturers to reduce their prices in order to recoup the capital invested in the merchandise.

The pricing of garments has two stages: price evaluation and bracketing prices.

Price evaluation

A conventional costing, while providing a calculated selling price, does not necessarily reflect the actual sales value of the garment itself. The need to apply a subjective evaluation of selling prices arises when the prices of similar garments in the
collection are compared.

For example, jacket A is priced at £30 and looks good value for money. Jacket
B is also priced at £30 but looks overpriced in relation to jacket A. The following
questions arise:

- Can the price of jacket A be raised to show the difference in apparent value?
- Should the price of jacket B be lowered to make it a more saleable
  proposition?
- If the prices were left unchanged, would this enhance the sales of jacket A?
- Finally, is there any commercial or other justification for retaining jacket B in
  the collection?

The selling prices of garments in the collection must reflect their comparative
values, and sometimes it is necessary to use subjective evaluations rather than take
the calculated price as 'gospel'.

Bracketing prices

Another example of the calculated costing for a garment being used only as a guide
is when the company is selling according to the price brackets of the retailer.

Most buyers for large groups work according to retail selling price categories
for particular types of merchandise in order to cover the relevant sectors of the
market which they serve. For example, the retail price categories for, say, ladies
dresses could be:

Bargain	£25 to £30
Cheap	£45 to £50
Average	£55 to £60
Expensive	£70 to £90
Luxury	>£90

This means that the price the buyer would be willing to pay the manufacturer for
a particular category of dress has to be at a level that slots into the appropriate
retail price category when the gross profit is added.

Retail gross profit margins on regular, as against sales, merchandise would vary
according to the degree of risk taken in purchasing. Fad fashions which become
out of date overnight are high-risk items and the retailer would work on considerably higher margins than for 'safe' garments.

Knowing this, the manufacturer will adjust the prices of individual garments up
or down to fit into the buyer's price range for this type and quality of garment.
When using this type of price juggling, the manufacturer will be aware of the

danger that a garment with a lowered price might turn out to be a winning style, but this risk is part and parcel of the clothing business.

Product planning

This is the process of determining the type and variety of garments to be produced by the company. In traditional economies, the types of clothing produced undergo very little change over a long period. However, as economies expand, the range of clothing products tends to increase and changes occur in the products themselves.

To paraphrase Bertrand Frank, this is the age of multiple wardrobes, with most people in developed countries owning several types of garment 'families', such as formal clothes, work clothes, rainwear, sportswear and leisure wear (14). Most of this assortment will be replaced or added to as fashions change and new types of products come on to the market.

This wide range of products enables a clothing company to find its own niche in a specific sector of the market by doing what it does best. This means exploiting to the maximum the inherent strength of the company whether this lies in design, response, flexibility, quality or price. Apart from being the age of multiple wardrobes, it has also been for a far longer time the age of specialisation.

Customers

The types of retail and wholesale organisations which are buyers of clothing are:

- *Department stores* Large retail units which sell a wide variety of products including clothing and fashion accessories.
- *Speciality department stores* Also large retail units, which sell clothing and accessories only. Both these types of department stores can be operated as independent units or may be part of a chain of similar units.
- *Chain stores* This is the name given to a retailing organisation operating a number of shops or speciality stores. Together, the larger chain store groups dominate the retailing and manufacturing sectors of the clothing business.
- *Supermarkets* Large purchasers of staple garments, such as underwear and hosiery and, increasingly, fashion items.
- *Co-operatives* These organisations are similar to chain stores.
- *Mail-order* Garments are sold directly from a mass-mailed catalogue. Retail mail-order selling was originally developed for rural customers, but now includes urban areas as well.
- *Independent shops* These are shops operating as individual units and sometimes specialising in one clothing category only, such as teenage fashions or outsizes.
- *Speciality wholesalers* These organisations purchase from manufacturers and re-sell to small retail units in outlying districts. They usually operate in areas where the clothing producers cannot support a sales force.

The types of customer served by a clothing company are determined by:

(1) *Scale* As a general rule large buyers require large suppliers, so the big manufacturing organisations will be closely related to these customers. Small, versatile producers specialise more in supplying the smaller retailer.

(2) *Peaks* Historically there are two production peaks during the year, with lulls in between; however, with the rapidity of style change encountered today these peaks may be more frequent but lower. The mail-order houses fill the lulls by placing orders far in advance of the season. They are very substantial purchasers but at keen prices, so only the large and efficient producers can supply their requirements. Thus the smaller producers of clothing experience the fluctuations of production levels far more severely than the big manufacturing organisations.

Distribution

This is the second major element of marketing and is involved with the physical movement of merchandise from the factory warehouse to the retailers' shops and/or central stores. Most clothing companies use what are called direct channels of distribution whereby goods are delivered to the retailers' premises or their nominated sub-distributors, without going through the hands of a second commercial party such as a wholesaler.

Apart from the physical distribution of goods, the merchandising section of the marketing department is also responsible for:

- the warehousing of finished goods;
- allocating customers' orders;
- packing the orders when necessary;
- deciding on the appropriate methods of transportation such as sea or air containers, hanging goods services, parcel services or the company's own transport and delivery facilities;
- continuous inventory control;
- ensuring that garments are delivered with a fresh and attractive appearance.

The efficient distribution of merchandise is an essential service and has an important influence on the company's image to its customers.

Sales

Promotion

The third element of marketing is sales promotion. This is aimed at motivating retailers and public alike to purchase merchandise produced under a specific brand or designer name. Systematic and well-planned promotion establishes the company's image, which in turn can lead to the generation of increased sales and the enhancement of other marketing functions.

Promotion is based on effective communication. The four channels of communication used for this are:

(1) *Advertising* This is the non-personal presentation of goods by an identifiable and associative name. Some of the mediums used for advertising are newspapers, magazines, posters, films, radio and television.
(2) *Publicity* This is directed more towards obtaining favourable media coverage that is not seen to be sponsored by the company concerned. A typical example could be where some prominent person is shown on television wearing a garment associated with the company.
(3) *Personal selling* One-to-one selling has been described in the introduction to this chapter and its importance should not be underestimated in the promotion of sales.
(4) *Presentations* Fashion shows for retailers or presented under the aegis of retailers are also important promotional activities.

In total, sales promotion attracts retailers and the general public, and builds and maintains brand loyalty.

Market research

Market research is another activity of the marketing department. This aspect of marketing deals with the gathering, processing and presentation of information which will serve as the basis for future decisions and planning. Research projects can be undertaken by the company's staff or by outside consultants, and these projects may be on any marketing subject.

Some of the objectives of market research are to determine:

- the market potential in a particular geographical area;
- what share of a market might be achieved;
- the characteristics of a given market;
- the distribution requirements for the market concerned;
- whether it is necessary to divide a market into separate territories;
- the organisation and staff required to service the market;
- the viability of selling through the company's own staff or through agents.

Market research can be conducted on a formal or an informal basis, and like every other kind of research requires objectivity, accuracy and thoroughness if the information derived from the study is to have any value as an aid to decision making.

Selling

The actual selling of a company's products can be achieved through the following channels:

(1) *Showroom-based staff*   These are sales personnel employed by the company and working in centrally located showrooms. They serve visiting customers and call on major customers.
(2) *Representatives*   Unlike the showroom sales staff, representatives visit all their customers at their own premises and generally deal with smaller retailers.
(3) *Agents*   These are independent selling organisations who can represent a number of manufacturers producing non-competing types of merchandise. Agents usually have their own showrooms and employ representatives. An agency could be granted exclusive selling rights for a particular region or an entire country.

The selling activities of a company which sells forward (takes advance orders) are concentrated into a very short period some months before the season. At this time established and potential customers are invited to the fashion shows which the manufacturer presents independently or in conjunction with other manufacturers. A large proportion of the company's sales volume is generated at this time, while sales made during the season are usually repeat orders for styles which have been successful.

Companies which sell from stock, as against those which take forward orders, usually hold their fashion shows very near the start of the season. These later shows enable customers to evaluate the market and buy for ex-stock delivery, rather than ordering merchandise three or four months in advance.

Sales forecasting and budgeting

The sales budget for a season is derived from the sales forecast and its preparation is a highly important function of the marketing department. The sales forecast provides the basis for all other planning and therefore must be as accurate as possible. In building up the sales budget, two related forecasts have to be made:

(1) The forecast selling prices of the different categories of garments in the final collection. While these prices have been calculated, they still retain an element of forecasting until customers' reactions to the pricing policy have been received.
(2) The forecast volume of sales for each category of product. Figure 6.1 shows an example of a sales forecast for a manufacturer producing merchandise in three price categories for the export and home markets.

The sales forecast is also a key document for the production and operations departments, because as well as forecasting the quantity of sales it details the anticipated dates for the initial bulk deliveries of merchandise. This information provides both these departments with the basis for preparing their own advance programmes.

Sales forecast		Season *Spring* Product *Skirts*		
Customers		Product Groups		
		A	B	C
Export	Home	Price *12.00*	Price *13.50*	Price *15.00*
Neal		4 000	8 000	
Caron			6 000	1 000
Daling			12 000	
Fenner		3 000	5 000	2 000
Cenda		2 000	3 000	1 000
Others		2 000	2 000	1 000
	Haro	1 000	2 000	
	Mattel	1 000	2 000	500
	Webster	500	1 000	250
	Cassy	1 000	2 500	750
	Others	1 000	3 000	1 000
Total units		15 500	46 000	7 500
Total value		186 000	621 000	112 500
Total sales	Units	69 000		
	Value	919 500		

Fig. 6.1 Sales forecast

To sum up

The marketing department plays a decisive role in determining the overall and detailed selling strategy of a clothing company. This is a highly responsible function because the implementation of marketing strategy, together with the attainment of the forecast sales, is central to the profitability of the company.

7 Finance Department

Introduction

The finance department is responsible for managing all the financial and adminis-trative affairs of the company and has a very important influence on many of the policy and commercial decisions taken by management.

The financing of a company's operations requires very precise, timely planning and control in order to ensure that adequate funds and credits are available when needed. Apart from the money to pay suppliers, salaries expenses, etc., funds have to be on hand to finance stocks of raw materials and finished goods and also the credit lines extended to customers. In the volatile clothing industry some provision also has to be made to cover periods when trading is difficult and revenues are down. Some of the more important functions performed by this department are:

- providing management information;
- budgeting;
- garment costings;
- administration.

Management information

In the world of business, success or failure is ultimately measured by money and therefore it is essential that the financial pulse of the company is subject to con-tinual measurement. The finance department is directly responsible for providing management with up-to-date information on the current and future financial status of the company.

The department will collect and collate financial and other statistical data and present it in a form which enables management to take more effective decisions. This information is gathered methodically and presented on a consistent basis, in reports covering every aspect of the company's activities. Some typical reports prepared for management are:

- monthly and cumulative balance sheets;
- stock levels and values;
- production costs;
- operating statements for the different departments in the company;
- cost of rejects and returns.

The information in these and other reports provides vital tools for management, and as Robert Appelby writes in *Figures Help* (23):

> 'Management information should help good managers to manage better but it is unlikely by itself to make bad managers efficient.'

Budgeting

The object of budgeting is to plan and control the company's activities so as to maximise profitability, and the starting point for all budgeting is the sales budget.

Sales budget

This budget is usually drawn up before the beginning of each new financial year or season and takes into account:

(1) the anticipated sales to the company's established customers;
(2) potential sales to new customers and to those who are in the process of building up their business volume with the company;
(3) the competitive strength of the company's products as compared with rival products;
(4) general economic trends at home and abroad;
(5) the manufacturing or sourcing capacity of the company;
(6) the availability of finance.

Figure 7.1 shows an example of a sales budget, but no special significance should be attached to the level of profitability shown in relation to sales because this would obviously vary according to the nature of the business. Most of the information required to prepare this budget would be supplied by the marketing department via their sales forecast. This forecast is not a commitment but rather a plan which gives a realistic direction before sales have actually been made.

Other budgets

The company's operational costs also need to be budgeted for, and these are typically:

Budget Forecast – period 1.9 to 31.12	
Forecast sales	Forecast costs
Home Market 420 000 Exports 150 000 Total 570 000	Materials 260 000 Labour 117 000 Overheads 132 000 Total 509 000

Forecast sales	570 000
Forecast costs	509 000
Forecast Profit	61 000

Fig. 7.1 Sales budget

(1) *Labour costs*   When an outline production forecast is available, the labour content of each garment is multiplied by the anticipated production to give the total cost of the direct labour requirements for the season.

(2) *Direct material costs*   These are derived from the sales budget, and costs are based on the forecast or known prices of raw materials. This budget is particularly important for planning the cash flow of the business in order to ensure that money will be available to pay suppliers on time.

(3) *Fixed overheads*   These are costs which have to be paid irrespective of whether facilities and staff are utilised, and among others they include:

- rent of buildings;
- rates payable to local authorities;
- insurance of factory property and machinery;
- depreciation charges on buildings;
- salaries of managers and principal officials;
- interest on capital.

(4) *Variable overheads*   These are costs which can vary according to production volume. Some examples are:

- energy of all kinds;
- maintenance;
- welfare;
- supervisors;
- clerical expenses;
- stationery, postage, telephones;
- holidays and sickness with pay.

(5) *Departmental budgets*   These budgets are prepared by the finance department in cooperation with the departments concerned and they serve as a basis for monitoring the actual costs as against the planned costs. Typical departmental budgets would be for:

- administration;
- marketing;
- distribution;
- production;
- purchasing.

Two of the most important functions of management are to plan the activities of the business and to evaluate the performance both of the company as a whole and of the individual managers working in the company. Budgets are the basis of all financial planning and monitoring systems.

Garment costings (bill of materials)

The costing is the 'identity card' of the garment and contains all the information required for the pre-production and production stages of making the garment. The costing sheet shows the detailed costs for:

- materials;
- labour;
- fixed and variable overheads;
- other expenses.

When these costs are combined they give the total cost price of the garment. Cost is important not only for determining the selling price but also for determining whether or not the garments can be made and sold at a profit – in effect, what the market is prepared to pay as against what the garment costs. Figure 7.2 shows a typical garment costing. (The figures used are for example purposes only.)

The information for the garment costing comes from various sources within the factory; for example:

- The sample section, cutting room or computerised marker planning unit provides details of the materials and trimmings required.
- A breakdown of the time values and costs involved in cutting, sewing and finishing the garment is supplied by the production engineering section.
- Materials and trimmings costs come from the purchasing department.
- The apportionment of fixed and variable overheads is determined by the finance department.

The actual costing itself is prepared by a specialist function in the finance department and then presented to the management for approval.

Garment costing				
Style no.	Description	Season	Sizes	Date
4929	Jacket	Winter	34–42	16/4

Item	Type	Quantity	Price	Unit price
Cloth	1616–100% wool	1.5m	9.0	13.50
Lining	207–100% viscose	1.2m	4.0	4.80
Fusibles	606	0.8m	3.0	2.40
Buttons	624–size 32	4	0.15	0.60
Zip				
Threads	Regular			0.50
Labels	1) Wool 1) Cleaning	1 + 1	0.05	0.10
Hanger	MT8	1	0.15	0.15
Packing	Bag 80 × 60	1	0.05	0.05

Production	Min.	Price	Cost		
				Total Materials	22.10
Cutting	8.0	0.16	1.28	Production	15.00
Sewing	50.0	0.14	7.00	General expenses	14.90
Pressing	6.0	0.15	0.90	Factory cost	52.00
Finishing	4.0	0.14	0.56	Profit	7.80
Inspection	4.0	0.15	0.60	Commission	3.14
Packing	3.0	0.14	0.42	Total cost	62.94
Totals	75.0		10.76	Selling price	63.00
Production Overhead			4.24	Approved by	
Total production cost			15.00		

Fig. 7.2 Garment costing

Garment costing in an outsourcing situation

It must be recognised that the majority of mass garment manufacture in the UK has gone offshore over the last 10 to 20 years. The main reason for this is to take advantage of low labour costs in emerging economies and thus source the production of garments more cheaply. Countries like Sri Lanka, India, Bangladesh, Taiwan and now mainland China have all become prominent in clothing manufacture.

This change in the way garments are sourced inevitably changes the nature of the costs involved. Sourcing companies do not have to be too concerned with the costing of the garments in the factory as they will usually negotiate an ex-factory price for the garments. Their concern will be the logistical costs of ensuring that the garments arrive back in the UK on the correct date and are of a suitable quality. The following list outlines the costs that may be incurred in a sourcing situation:

- ex-factory price of garments;
- costs relating to sourcing fabrics and accessories for production;

- costs relating to maintaining quality control in a remote location;
- shipping or air-freight costs;
- tariffs;
- insurance in transit;
- warehousing both in the remote location and in the UK;
- pre-distribution maintenance of garments to ensure quality.

Thus in a sourcing situation the ex-factory costs of the garments may be very low but the overhead costs are increased.

Administration

Another aspect of the finance department's work is concerned with administration, which covers a wide range of subjects.

All the departments in a clothing company require administrative support for their operations to ensure that affairs are dealt with in an orderly and systematic fashion. To this end, procedures are established for all the routine activities necessary to keep the business running smoothly. These procedures include:

- preparing orders to suppliers;
- checking goods inwards;
- timing and methods of stocktaking;
- imports and exports;
- obtaining credits for returned goods and materials;
- issuing credits for customer returns;
- negotiating and issuing tenders for major projects;
- purchasing office furniture and equipment.

A clothing business has 'up-front' departments such as design, marketing and production/sourcing, and the fact that they can function smoothly is generally the result of good administrative support in the background.

To sum up

The levels of financial planning and control and administrative organisation are important contributory factors to the success or otherwise of a business. Although the work of the finance department is sometimes associated with paper-pushing, it is an essential part of the organisation.

8 Purchasing Department

The primary objective of the purchasing department is to obtain the right materials, in the right quantity, at the right time and price. Since purchased materials are the largest component in the cost of a garment, purchasing is an extremely important and specialist function within a clothing company. As the purchasing department and raw materials stores are operational departments, they are in most organisations responsible to the operations manager, while the management of the finished goods warehouse is responsible to the marketing department.

The main functions of the purchasing department are described in the rest of this chapter.

Information

The purchasing office is the company's 'window on the world' and provides information to all concerned regarding new products, materials and services. While all materials having a fashion element are screened and selected by the design department, there are a host of other materials and products about which the management team requires ongoing information. The specialist functions in the company usually have their own sources of information but the purchasing department helps them find alternative suppliers or trace specific items not carried by their regular suppliers.

Suppliers

The approval of a product and its price is normally given by the department for whom the product is intended, but the purchasing department must ensure that the supplier is stable and reliable. This is particularly important where a new supplier does not have a known track record. A delivery commitment which cannot be fulfilled by the manufacturing unit because of the late delivery or serious quality faults of a material from one of their suppliers can have very expensive repercussions for the company.

Prices

While the price, quality and quantity of materials are usually specified by the operations department, the purchase must be made at the most advantageous terms for the company. Other terms and conditions such as freight costs, insurance, discounts and credit terms are also negotiated before the order is placed. In particular, the credit terms negotiated with suppliers are an important factor in planning the cash flow of the company for a specific period.

Progressing

This is concerned with ensuring that the ordered materials arrive at the correct time, and the purchasing department will invest a lot of effort in making sure that the production plan for the factory can be executed without any hold-ups caused by the late or non-delivery of raw materials.

The system employed to progress orders can be manual or computerized, and is basically a diary detailing the orders placed and their confirmed delivery dates. Figure 8.1 shows the principles of this progressing diary where the deliveries are marked off as and when they are received, and in the case of split deliveries the balances continue to be progressed in the same way. A responsibility of progressing is to verify with suppliers and shippers that delivery schedules are being maintained as planned. If it becomes evident that certain materials will not arrive on

			Order Details			Receipts			Balances			
Supplier	Order Number	Date	Quan	Colour	Delivery	Date	Quan	Del Note	Quan	Expected	Delivered	Del Note
Dillon	11712	28 4	500m	Red	30/6	28/6	505	4128		Complete		
			400m	Green			410					
			200m	White			202					
			1100m				1117m					
Dillon	11789	10/5	1000m	Blue	15/7	10/7	600	4884	400	15/7	17/7	4921
			800m	Orange			810	4884		Complete		
			1800m				1410m		400			
Dillon	11801	20/5	600m	Silver	30/7							
			600m									

Fig. 8.1   Order progressing

time, the purchasing office will inform the production planning section so that production can be rescheduled.

Verification

In well-managed businesses, a standard procedure is to check that prices, quantities, colours, etc. of delivered materials agree with the particulars specified in the purchase order. The storekeeper checks quantities and the materials are then inspected by quality assurance personnel. If everything is found to be in order, the purchasing department approves the supplier's invoice for payment on the due date.

Speculative buying

When market conditions are particularly favourable, the purchasing department may recommend ordering materials such as fusibles, linings and sewing threads which are not required for immediate use. This type of purchasing is justifiable if there are indications that standard types of raw materials are likely to become difficult to obtain, or that the price will rise sharply. In many cases this would apply to imported materials where possible currency devaluations or rises in foreign currency rates could significantly affect the cost to the company.

Storekeeping

The storekeeping staff are basically responsible for the receiving, storage and issuing of materials. The chief storekeeper is expected to:

- Receive goods inwards and check them according to procedures specified by the purchasing department.
- Store the goods so that no deterioration or damage occurs through, say, exposure to sunlight or crushing. Linings will change colour very quickly if exposed to continuous harsh light, while delicate pile fabrics can be severely damaged if crushed by being stored in cramped conditions.
- Issue the materials and trimmings according to calculated amounts rather than by rounded-up figures which are sometimes more convenient to handle. For instance, a requisition for 120 buttons could be easily supplied by issuing a unit pack of one gross, but this would encourage waste as well as possibly creating shortages.

Stock management

The management of the raw materials and technical stores is expected to maintain and provide accurate and up-to-date information on the stock levels of all items carried. This information is essential for the purchasing department because it dictates the frequency and type of order placed with suppliers. Where the materials management systems are computerised, the data is automatically available to the purchasing department who will issue one of two types of purchase order:

(1) *One-time order*   This is an order for a material or trim which will not usually be repeated; for example, an order for a batch of cloth to be used for one style only.

 Because of short lead times, fashion cloths are not usually stock items with mills or cloth merchants except in cases where they are holding a back-up stock in anticipation of repeat orders. Most clothing factories place a single order for all their requirements of one cloth and may request a split delivery, i.e. part on one date and the balance on another date. The quantities and timings of deliveries relate to the production plan, which helps the company with both storage space and payments.

(2) *Stock level orders*   These are placed for items used by the factory all the year round where a minimum stock level has to be maintained. These items include stationery, pins, chalk, pattern paper and high-mortality spares for sewing machines.

 The ordering system itself is based on the predetermined minimum and maximum stock levels for each item; a fixed point between these two levels indicates when a further supply should be ordered, with the idea that by the time the ordered goods are received, the stock should have fallen to approximately the minimum level. The absolute reserve is the difference between the minimum stock level and zero stock.

 A common variation of this type of order is where, because of advantageous terms or price hedging, a company orders a full year's requirement of a particular item but requests the supplier to deliver at a periodic rate roughly equal to the consumption rate of the factory.

Purchase order

This is the means by which the company places orders with suppliers and is an important contractual document which could bind the company to considerable expenditure. It is therefore most important that the purchase order is clear and unambiguous and does not use terms such as 'Price to be agreed', 'Delivery as soon as possible' or 'As discussed', which are too loose to be of any use if there are disagreements with the supplier. Figure 8.2 shows an example of a purchase order with the type of information required to prevent possible misunderstandings with suppliers. The purchase order should also ideally include information for the use of other departments within the company. Immediately after the issue of the signed order to the supplier, the details are entered into the planning, progressing and stock management systems so that the information is available to all concerned.

Fastline Fashions Ltd. 382 Gt. Portfield Street London	Order no.	11704
	Date	16/4
	Category	RM-F
To: *Revin Fusibles Ltd.* *Wigan*	Re: Your quotation	
	Number	2028
	Date	10/4

We order as follows:

No.	Quantity	Description	Unit price	Total
1	500 m	Fusible 464 white	1.10 m	550
2	300 m	grey	1.10 m	330
3	200 m	black	1.10 m	220
	1000 m			
		All 90 cm width		
			Total	1100

Delivery	Transport	Payment	Budget
15/5	Yours	45 days	64F

Comments	Ordered by	Approved by
In one delivery		

Please quote this order number on all documents

Fig. 8.2 Purchase order

To sum up

The purchasing department is the biggest money spender within the company and as such has a great deal of responsibility, not only for logistics but also for controlling expenditure. Good profits start with good buying.

9 Production Department

In a small unsophisticated factory such as an outside contractor, the owner and/or the production manager is responsible for all activities within the factory, which include:

- output of the factory;
- garment quality;
- working methods and technology;
- materials and trim purchasing;
- labour recruitment and training.

This type of organisation is usually very effective when the product range is kept small and the products themselves are relatively simple. Apart from directing the production activities, the management is involved in the day-to-day administrative work required to keep the factory running. Overheads have to be kept to the absolute minimum and specialised services are provided by external agencies such as sewing machine mechanics, general maintenance services and accountants.

As production becomes more complex, the knowledge necessary for the detailed management of a large production department is beyond the ability of one person. Consequently specialist functions are created to provide the depth of knowledge required and to narrow the fields of responsibility.

In a larger, more sophisticated environment the production department has three main groups of functions: manufacturing, service and control.

Manufacturing functions

These are concerned with the actual production of garments and include:

- *Cutting room*   Here all the processes required to turn piece goods into cut garments are performed.

- *Sewing room* Apart from actual sewing this includes operations such as fusing, under-pressing and in-process inspection. Sometimes the sewing room will use outside contractors for operations which the factory is not equipped to carry out, such as pleating, embroidery and quilting.
- *Pressing room* This department gives the garment its final finish by a process called top-pressing.
- *Finishing* After top-pressing, this section performs operations such as button sewing, and attaching labels and hangtags.
- *Final inspection* Although this is not strictly a production function, it is tied in with production because the inspection department gives the 'go' or 'no-go' for every garment produced.
- *Packing* Before entering the finished goods warehouse, garments such as shirts and underwear are boxed while hanging goods such as skirts are bagged.

Service functions

While the service sections mainly assist the production department, they also extend their services to other departments within the organisation. The main service departments are production engineering, personnel and training, machinery and equipment maintenance, general maintenance and technical stores.

Production engineering

This section has two main areas of activity: the staff function and the line function.

The staff function

Here production engineering is concerned with project planning and development and many other behind-the-scenes activities necessary to achieve the current and future objectives of the factory.

The line function

As the name suggests, this function deals with the day-to-day applications of production engineering in the factory itself. Among others, these applications include work study, premium schemes and following up the results of technological or other changes.

Personnel and training

While the personnel officer is responsible for recruiting staff, the bulk of the training provided is aimed at ensuring that the production department has the required flow of trained operators.

Machinery and equipment maintenance

This is a highly specialised section which deals with the repair, maintenance and running-in of all the machinery and equipment used by the production department. Apart from sewing machines, this includes cutting and spreading machines, pressing machines and transport systems.

General maintenance

The work of this section covers all the main services and utilities used by the entire company, including building maintenance, air conditioning, main power supplies and dealing with outside contractors for large projects and installations. The two maintenance sections usually work very closely together when major changes are being made to layouts or when very large items of production equipment are being installed.

Technical stores

Depending on the size of the company, there can be a general technical stores which holds all the items required for repairs and maintenance, or there can be specialist stores which carry parts and materials for specific end uses. Logically the stores for sewing machine parts is located as close as possible to the repair shop, which in turn is close to the main production area. Building materials and pipe stores are more conveniently situated on a perimeter road where they can receive and handle bulky deliveries.

Control functions

These cover control services which provide production management with regular and up-to-date information on the overall and detailed performance of the factory. This information flow helps those responsible for production keep their fingers on the pulse and enables them to anticipate and correct deviations from plans. The main control functions are as follows.

Production planning and control

Working from the overall production plans of the operations department, the planning and control staff of the production department prepare micro-production plans. As these plans become operative, the control function operates feedback systems for measuring actual performance against planned performance.

The difference between the controls of the operations department and the production department is in scale. The operations department is interested in finished garments only, whereas the production department has to control every major stage of producing the garments up to their entry into the warehouse.

Budgetary control

As discussed in Chapter 7, budgets are set for each department in the company and the finance department provides regular reports regarding the plus or minus variances from the planned costs. These reports are of particular importance to the production department because, after raw materials, production labour, overheads and facilities are together usually the second largest component in the cost price of a garment.

Quality control

There has always been some discussion on whether garment quality control belongs to production management or whether it should be an independent activity. But however the control is organised, production management needs immediate information regarding the slightest deviations from standards because any delay in discovering and rectifying quality problems can have serious results for the company. Production management requires quality reports as well as other reports from the control functions, to ensure that quantity and quality of output go hand in hand.

To sum up

This section outlines the major elements and associated functions of the production department. In Part 3, the main aspects of manufacturing technology will be examined in more detail.

10 Operations Department

'Operations department' is one of the names given to the department that has the overall responsibility for planning, controlling and coordinating all activities concerned with the logistics of raw materials supply and the production of garments.

Company calendar

The starting point for operations planning is the company calendar which sets out the chronological sequence and duration of activities needed to ensure that the company will have merchandise ready at the right times during the year. In practice, the company calendar is the master plan for the entire company and is used by each department to develop its own plans. It is central to all planning, and some of the major considerations which influence its construction are examined here.

The seasons

The overall operation of a clothing company producing garments that are staple or semi-styled has a fixed cycle which is dictated by the unchanging sequence and durations of the seasons. For clothing manufacturers this means that certain deadlines have to be met if merchandise is to reach retailers at the right time to meet the seasonal demands of the general public.

For many years, most of the clothing industry worked on a three-phase year which covered the four seasons as follows: *Phase 1* Spring merchandise; *Phase 2* Summer merchandise; *Phase 3* Combined autumn and winter merchandise. Retailers would place advance orders for merchandise which would be on display for the duration of the season.

A more recent selling pattern is to have three seasons during the year, with each season divided into two phases so as to introduce new merchandise to the public during the season. This pattern is:

Spring 1   Spring merchandise
Spring 2   Late spring and early summer merchandise
Summer 1   Summer merchandise
Summer 2   Late summer and early autumn merchandise
Winter 1   Autumn and early winter merchandise
Winter 2   Winter merchandise

The recently labelled phenomenon of 'fast-fashion' often attracts talk of a season-less approach to fashion retail, and consequently to manufacturing; however, a more accurate description would illustrate frequent product variations within micro-seasons.

While seasons can vary in duration, the basic pattern of retail sales is seasonal and this is what controls most of the clothing industry. Figure 10.1 shows the selling periods and peaks of each season, together with the slight overlaps between them. The lulls between seasons are used for the Sales, usually in January and July, and these provide retailers and manufacturers with the opportunity to dispose of unsold stocks. It sometimes happens after a boom season that merchandise has to be produced especially for the Sales, which generates additional turnover for retailers, manufacturers and cloth suppliers.

Therefore, when preparing a company calendar, the first stage is to establish the link between seasonal retail sales and garment production. The first question to ask is when the public will expect to find merchandise for a particular season available in the shops. For example, the British public expects to find winter clothes in the shops from about the beginning of September and a small amount of buying starts around this time. This builds up to a peak at about the end of October and then gradually tapers off to a finish by the middle of December.

Consequently, the retailer expects to receive initial orders of winter merchandise between the middle and end of August and the completion of advance orders by the first or second week of October. The advance orders usually represent only

Fig. 10.1 Seasonal sales pattern

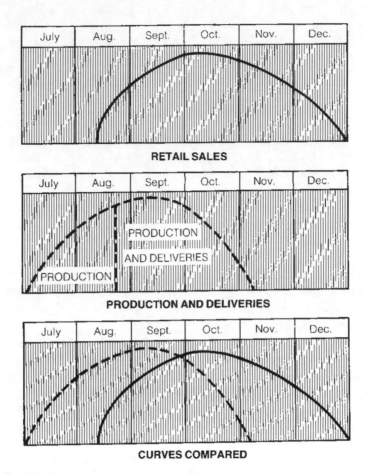

Fig. 10.2   Retail sales and production

part of the purchases for the season, with the remaining supplies coming from repeat orders and/or buying from stock houses.

So it is apparent that there is a difference in phasing between retail and production peaks, and this difference, for the winter season, is shown in Figure 10.2. The production phase only shows when garments are being produced and delivered but does not detail all the other events which have to be completed before production begins. Therefore the next stage in formulating the company calendar is to work backwards from the commencement of production to establish what has to happen and when to enable the factory to start production at the correct time.

The time axis

According to J.A. Blackburn, the process of producing cloths for a new season starts some 15 to 18 months before the garments are actually delivered to the retailers (1). (Note that even for 'fast-fashion' fabric production lead times are still of this order.) Part of this period, when interpolated with the production phase of a season, becomes the timescale along which the clothing industry has to operate.

The basis of all production planning is having raw materials available at the right time, and the most important of these materials is top cloth. There are two sides to this: the mills and the clothing manufacturer.

The mills

According to various texts on the subject, the timetable for producing cloth for a particular season is:

Month 1	Design fabrics
Month 3	Order yarns for sample ranges
Month 5	Make sample range collections
Month 7	Show sample range to customers
Month 8	Produce sample lengths or pieces for customers
Month 9	Deliver samples to customers
Months 10 and 11	The customer is sampling and selling
Months 12–13 and 14	Produce and deliver bulk orders

From the design of the cloth to the delivery of bulk orders takes 13 to 14 months, and if the production time up to delivery is added, then 15 to 18 months is not an exaggeration.

Another important fact which emerges from this timetable is that the clothing manufacturer became involved in month 7 and starts to receive bulk deliveries about four or five months afterwards. So month 7 is another key point in the company calendar.

The clothing manufacturer

Depending on the type of business, the clothing manufacturer will place bulk orders with mills or merchants by one of the following methods:

• Buying for stock without having orders in hand. This is a strategy perhaps best suited to fast-fashion producers, enabling them to avoid the prolonged fabric development lead time.
• Buying against orders, plus additional amounts for making up stock or repeat orders.
• Large-scale manufacturers who work exclusively for one retail chain usually develop fabrics with their customer and the mill. They order the phasing of cloth deliveries according to their relatively long-term production programmes.
• Name designer houses who generate their own garment designs work very closely with the more exclusive textile producers and so are not in the same position as most other clothing manufacturers. In some cases, the name houses are backed by large textile concerns who use the designer's name and work to

showcase their products. This provides both parties with the benefits of being part of a vertical organisation.

Another aspect of raw materials supplies is that concerned with auxiliary materials which have to be cut, and trimmings of all types.

Linings are usually held in stock by the converter in grey cloth (loomstate form) or as finished products in standard colours, and can be supplied at reasonably short notice. Fusible interlinings, generally called fusibles, very rarely have a fashion element except when there is a need for a special colour. The great majority of fusible producers manufacture their basic products on a continuous basis and can also deliver at fairly short notice.

The manufacturer either works from hand to mouth by buying linings and fusibles from stock, or places bulk orders well in advance for the materials to be delivered in specified quantities at fixed intervals during the manufacturing season. The second method not only ensures continuity of supply but also has price advantages.

Other trimmings such as buttons, zips and sewing threads are either available from stock in standard colours or can be coloured up and delivered fairly quickly. When possible, clothing manufacturers usually provide their trimmings suppliers with an indication of types, colours and quantities some time in advance so that adequate stocks will be available when required.

Regardless of the size and operational style of the clothing company, the precise timing of ordering and receiving raw materials is vital.

The timing of activities

Apart from production periods which are linked to raw material deliveries, another series of events has to take place so that the company will be in a position to place bulk orders for cloths. For a company mainly producing against orders, the sequence and approximate duration of these events for a typical season is shown in Table 10.1.

Bulk deliveries of materials will start six to eight weeks after the orders have been placed with the mills. All in all, five to six months has elapsed from the time

Table 10.1 Typical sequence of pre-ordering events

Department	Activity	Duration (weeks)
Design	Visits to fashion and textile shows	3–4
Design	Make initial core samples	3–4
Design	Make collection samples	3–4
Marketing	Sales	3–4
Operations	Order materials	2
	Total approx.	14–18

Winter season														
Department	Activity	Month												
		1	2	3	4	5	6	7	8	9	10	11	12	
Design	Plan and design collection		▲											
Design	Make patterns and samples			▲										
Marketing	Forward sales				▲									
Purchasing	Order raw materials					▲								
Design	Grade patterns					▲								
Purchasing	Receive raw materials								▰					
Production	Produce customer's orders									▰				
Marketing	Distribute to customers									▰				
	Retail sales										▲			

Fig. 10.3 Company calendar

the designer started thinking about the collection to the time the factory starts producing the new styles. This routine takes place at least twice a year, and obviously each event must be completed in its right sequence and at the right time for the factory to deliver on time.

Figure 10.3 shows an example of a company calendar which contains the main elements of sampling, sales, production and delivery of winter merchandise for the English market. The timing and duration of events can vary from company to company but they must all go through the same procedures if they are to have merchandise ready to deliver on time.

> **To sum up**
>
> The company calendar provides an overall plan for the whole factory and has its own built-in control system – the time-scale. The operations department uses the calendar for planning and controlling everything leading up to and including production.

Pre-production planning and control

This is a function within the operations department which plans and controls all the activities leading up to the actual production of garments. In effect, it is pre-production planning and control which organises and manages the route from the customer to the cutting room.

The overall objective is to ensure that the logistics of supply and production are planned in such a manner that:

(1) the sales programme is achieved on time;
(2) labour, machinery and other resources are utilised to the best advantage.

The main operations involved are described here.

Order concentration

Where the same range of sample garments is shown to a number of different customers, it is more than likely that there will be orders for the same garments from more than one of them. The individual orders for the same garments can be manufactured in one of two ways:

(1) By cutting and producing each customer's order separately.
(2) By cutting and producing together all orders for the same garment.

Obviously the second alternative is the most efficient because it enables the factory to work on longer runs of the same garments, with all the consequent benefits of producing larger batches. However, the combining of a number of individual orders is dependent on whether the delivery dates for all the orders are close enough to prevent the need for lengthy and expensive storage of finished garments. If this condition is fulfilled, then the orders can be cut and produced at the same time.

An important consideration when concentrating orders is whether the totals sold per size and colour provide balanced cuts in terms of the ratios between the quantities needed of different sizes. As ratio cutting is accepted to be the most efficient method of cutting, these totals are sometimes manipulated so as to provide more efficient cutting. This adjustment process involves the rounding up or down of the actual quantities sold in order to arrive at a simple ratio between the totals to be cut in each size. The order concentration shown in Figure 10.4 illustrates the principle of this process.

Another point to consider about size ratios is that there is a known distribution of sizes and quantities within each sector of the market. This ratio of distribution is used when retailers place orders so that the amounts ordered per size match the known selling pattern of those sizes. A stock house which produces merchandise in advance of receiving orders cuts its stock garments according to the size ratios of the market it serves.

Production block planning

On receiving orders the company generally issues an acknowledgment in which it confirms all the conditions of the order, especially that of the delivery date. To be able to confirm delivery dates, the production potential for any given period has to be known and set off against the garments to be produced within that period. This is called a block, or macro-plan, and is usually prepared to cover an entire season's production capacity. More detailed micro-plans are drawn up for shorter periods within the season by the planning staff of the production department.

Style no.	Description	Price	Cloth	Composition	Colours		Cloth type	Production time
7143	Jacket	38.50	1485	100% wool	Blue–orange pink		Plain	1.5 hrs.

Customer	Order number	Colour pink/11					Colour orange/14					Colour blue/17					Total	Delivery date
		36	38	40	42	44	36	38	40	42	44	36	38	40	42	44		
Caron	1641	9	16	25	16	9	10	25	35	30	15	10	16	35	21	10	282	30/9
Neal	20073	8	16	25	16	8	15	30	35	25	15	12	22	40	20	10	297	15/9
Daling	6377	8	19	25	16	8	15	26	49	25	10	8	19	15	21	10	274	30/9
Total sold		25	51	75	48	25	40	81	119	80	40	30	57	90	62	30	853	✓
Plus					2				1				3				6	✓
Minus			1					1							2		4	✓
Total to cut		25	50	75	50	25	40	80	120	80	40	30	60	90	60	30	855	✓
Size ratios		1	2	3	2	1	1	2	3	2	1	1	2	3	2	1		Approved by

Fig. 10.4 Order concentration

Block planning works on the following principles:

With small variations, factories are usually staffed and equipped according to the planned output level of the average type of garment produced. This means that the number of operators and the equipment for each group of operations is sufficient to perform the required number of operations per day. The various groups of operations are balanced with each other so that each section is capable of producing a similar amount of work during the same period of time.

Using the finalised order concentrations as the input, the block plan takes the projected work hours available and allocates them to the number of garments sold in each style and the time required to make each garment. This global calculation would be done on the basis of, say, a working month and would take into account the anticipated deliveries of raw materials and the total net working hours during that period. Thus a factory having a production staff of, say, 60 people, each of whom works 8 hours net a day, would have 480 production hours available for each full day worked during the month. Assuming that an average garment has a balanced work content of 1.5 hours, the anticipated production of this garment would be 320 units per day, i.e. 480 hours ÷ 1.5 hours. If the factory has an order for 1200 of this style, which for some reason are to be produced over a period of ten days, then for each of the ten days 180 hours (120 × 1.5) would be allocated to the production of this particular order. The production hours remaining for each day would in turn be allocated to the production of other orders. An example of this global planning technique is shown in Figure 10.5.

A well-maintained block plan, whether manual or computerised, provides management with up-to-date information regarding factory loading and delivery sched-

Block production programme						
Customer	Production order number	Style number	Week number			
			5	6	7	8
			Quantity	Quantity	Quantity	Quantity
Caron	1618	6142	310			
Neal	1618	6142	400			
Neal	1619	6150	300	300		
Caron	1619	6150		160		
Daling	1619	6150		250	250	
Fenner	1620	6149		300	200	200
Neal	1621	6147			120	100
Daling	1622	6143			150	160
Fenner	1622	6143			300	200
Daling	1623	6144				360
Totals			1010	1010	1020	1020

Fig. 10.5 Block planning

ules and enables them to make realistic commitments to customers. Apart from everything else, on-time deliveries are essential if a clothing company is to build up and maintain a reputation for reliability with its customers.

Raw materials

Parallel to the production planning activities, orders for raw materials are prepared. The information for placing these is derived from the garment costing and the order concentration totals for that particular garment.

The procedure is firstly to calculate the quantities of each item required and then to concentrate them if the same materials and colours are used for more than one style. The final quantities are then rounded off according to the average unit length of the particular material being ordered. For example, if the average length of a roll of lining is 100 metres, then it will be ordered in multiples of that length. Where the quantities are so small that the ordering of a complete roll is not justified, substitutions might be made or materials purchased from trimmings merchants at a higher price than that which would be paid to converters or mills.

Before issuing the orders for raw materials, a delivery schedule is prepared according to the production block plan. This is sent to suppliers, and it is only when they confirm that they can supply by the specified dates that the orders are placed. Obviously some allowances must be made in case suppliers do not deliver on time, so there will always be a slight element of overstocking to cover possible shortages and to maintain the continuity of production.

Raw materials supply is a highly critical function because considerable losses and delays can be incurred if half-completed garments have to be put aside because of late or incomplete deliveries of raw materials. A production order to the factory cannot really be considered effective unless all the raw materials and trimmings necessary to make the garments are to hand when the order is issued.

The production order

Up to this stage, all the information concerning the production of a particular batch of garments has been spread over a number of documents, including the costing, individual customers' orders and the order concentration. Now all this data has to be combined to provide information for the actual production of the garments. A production order is used to convey the compilations of the planning function to the production function. An example of a production order is shown in Figure 10.6, and in one form or another this is the document which sums up all the processes on the road from the customer to the cutting room.

Production order											No. 1676
Style no.	Quantity	Cloth	Type	Costings				Work entry		Delivery	Date issued
6152	315	804	Plain	Cloth 1.5m	Lining 1.0m	Fusible 0.5m	Fusible	Week no. 11		Week no. 14	10/3
Material	Product	Colour	Total	8	10	12	14	16	18	20	22	Total
Cloth	804	Orange/7	270m		20	40	60	40	20			180
		Pink/11	203m		15	30	45	30	15			135
Lining	1577	Orange	180m									
		Pink	135m									
Fusible	606	White	160m									
			Totals		35	70	105	70	35			315

Fig. 10.6 Production order

> **To sum up**
>
> The pre-production phase for an order or combination of orders can be said to have ended when the production order, graded patterns and all the raw materials are issued to the factory.

Production planning and control (PP & C)

This is probably the most important function provided to the production department because without it the department is like a bus driving along the road without a fixed route, destination or timetable.

PP & C can be a function of production engineering or, as is more usually the case, a unit within the operations department. Where production is dispersed over a number of locations, a central department is needed to collect and analyse the control information from each production unit in order to report on individual and overall achievements. In this situation, a central PP & C unit within the operations department would have an ideal overview position for making the changes sometimes necessary as a result of production or logistic problems.

Actual planning work starts when a production order, graded patterns and raw materials are ready to be issued to the factory by the operations department. The sequence and planning operations are:

- marker and cut planning;
- marker planning;
- cutting room production planning.

Marker and cut planning

This can be a manual or computerised technique and is used to determine:

- the minimum number and types of spreads required to cut the order;
- the composition of these spreads if different colours are to be cut together;
- the markers required for the spreads;
- whether original markers have to be created, or copies of existing markers can be used if the particular style has been cut previously.

The cut order plan for the production order in Table 10.2 is shown in Figure 10.7 and details the spreads and markers required for the top cloth.

As well as cut planning individual production orders, the planners try to concentrate cutting orders where the same materials are being used. This cut concentration mainly applies to trims such as fusibles, linings and pocketing where labour, materials or machinery utilisation could be improved by combining a number of orders.

Cut and marker planning finally produces details of the spreads and markers for the production orders planned for production during a given period, and these cut plans provide the basis for the next stage of marker planning.

Table 10.2 Production order

Production order no. 1160 Style no. 6144							Cloth type: plain
Colour	8	10	12	14	16	18	20	Total
Red	—	70	140	210	140	70	—	630
Green	—	40	80	90	50	10	—	270
Totals	—	110	220	300	190	80	—	900

Production order number: 1160										
Style	Quantity		Cloth	Nett width	Shrinkage		Spreading mode		Patterns	
6144	900		Plain	148 cm	L: 1.5%	W: 0.8%	Face up – One way		Paired one-way	

Spread number	Marker sizes					Marker number		Spreading			
	10	12	14	16	18	Original	Copy	Colour	Plys	Units	Total
1160/1	1	2	3	2	1	6144/2		Red	40	360	360
1160/2	1	2	3	2	1		6144/2	Red	30	270	360
	1	2	3	2	1			Green	10	90	
1160/3	1	2	2	1		6144/3		Green	30	180	180

Fig. 10.7 Cut order plan – top cloth

Marker planning

Working from the cut order plans, the supervisor of the marker planning unit allocates cut-orders to the various operatives who then plan the markers. (This subject is examined more fully in Chapter 11.)

Cutting room production planning

The inputs for this stage are the cut plans for individual production orders, which are used to prepare the production plan for the cutting room. Apart from the cut plans, three determinants must also be coordinated and combined into the work programme:

(1) The capacity of the cutting room to deal with a mixture of different types of cloths.
(2) Whether the best mixture for the cutting room is necessarily the best mixture for the sewing room.

(3)   If the mixture is suitable for the cutting and sewing rooms, is it in accordance
      with the delivery schedule of the company?

All these determinants can be combined in the best way possible either manually
or by a computerised algorithmic technique which produces, by means of a systematic mathematical procedure, the optimum solution to this multi-factor
problem. A more detailed look at these determinants follows.

Cutting room

There are three basic types of cloth which could be cut and each one has a direct
influence on the production levels which can be achieved by the cutting room.
These cloth types are:

(1)   Plain fabrics which do not require any special processing. Cutting production
      is at its highest when these are being processed.
(2)   Partial matching cloths with warp or weft stripes which require a certain
      amount of straightening and matching in order to ensure the symmetry and
      straightness of components. When handling these types of cloths, cutting pro-
      duction is somewhat lower than for plain fabrics.
(3)   Bold checked or traverse striped cloths are the bane of the cutting room because
      the garments cut from these fabrics usually have to be fully matched in every
      respect. Cutting production is at its lowest when working on this type of cloth.

A first planning consideration is whether the totals arrived at for the cutting
room are the same as those required to maintain full production in the sewing
room and, subsequently, the planned delivery schedule. This is not as simple as it
seems because a cloth which creates major production problems in the cutting
room could have far less effect on the output of the sewing room. So assuming
that the totals and mixture are acceptable for the cutting room, the next stage is
to extend the cutting room programme to the sewing room and verify whether the
proposed mixture of styles and cloths can be produced at the required rate. For
the sewing room, this would involve the consideration of cloths, style detail and
machinery and equipment.

Cloths
Garments cut in cloths that require matching are also a problem for the sewing
room and this would be taken into account by the management of the sewing room
when evaluating the proposed work programme. Apart from sewing problems,
certain types of cloths also create production problems because they require, for
example, special fusing conditions or extra care in pressing.

Style detail
While most garments produced in a factory contain a reasonable balance between
different operations, some styles can create serious imbalances between the different sections in a production unit.

For example, a man's jacket with single-breasted lapels, flapped pockets and no side vents is relatively easier to produce than a jacket with double-breasted lapels, patch pockets and two side vents. The production unit would obviously be set up to produce both styles of garment but the question is, what are the optimum levels for both styles if the production unit as a whole is to stay in balance? This is another problem which has to be solved when planning the production for a sewing room.

Machinery and equipment

Another limiting factor on output could be the maximum production obtainable from speciality sewing machines. Factories are normally equipped with a balanced mixture of regular, special and speciality machines which can adequately cope with the average combination and quantities of sewing operations for the range of garments produced. However, problems can arise if the quantity of garments requiring the use of speciality machines rises above the machines' capacities.

Management is not always in a position to prepare in advance for these eventualities because it is virtually impossible to pinpoint accurately the potential winners in a collection before the season. Therefore if a situation arises during the season where the production of a certain style is limited because of a speciality operation, production has to be planned accordingly.

Production plans

When the projected cutting room and sewing room production plans have been agreed on, two working plans are issued. The difference between them lies in the quantities produced by each of these sections. In operative terms this could mean that a spread for a certain style contains, say, 450 garments, but the sewing room requires them to be fed in at the rate of 150 per day for three days. So the spread of 450 garments would appear on the cutting room programme as part of one day's production while the same number of garments would be spread over three days of the sewing room programme.

Figure 10.8 shows an example of a cutting room programme for one day. It contains an inbuilt allowance for the total processing time needed for a batch from the time it enters the cutting room until it is available for issue to the sewing room. This programme is for top cloth only and similar ones would be made for linings, fusibles, etc.

The programme for a factory with three production units is illustrated in Figure 10.9. It would also take into account the amount of time required for garments to go through production and reach the finished goods warehouse. This allowance is called throughput-time and is based on the total number of garments in process and the average daily production rate of the factory.

If the factory has, for example, 5000 garments in work and the average rate of production is 500 units per day, then all things being equal, a garment will reach the warehouse 11 full working days after it has been issued from the cutting room.

Cutting programme – Top cloth							Date 23/5
Order number	Style number	Cloth type			Spread number	Quantity	Factory	Feed rate
		Plain	Stripe	Check				
4178	3022		✓		116	320	Leeds	300
4179	3023		✓		117	280	"	200
4180	3027	✓			126	450	"	250
4182	3028	✓			128	410	Wigan	300
4183	3031	✓			129	220	"	150
4185	3030			✓	131	150	Bradford	100
4186	3034	✓			136	200	"	200
					Total	2030	Total	1500

Fig. 10.8   Cutting room production programme

Week no 16			Working days 5					
Factory Leeds			Factory Wigan			Factory Bradford		
Order no	Style	Quan.	Order no	Style	Quan.	Order no	Style	Quan.
4188	3036	610	4192	3029	420	4197	3046	160
4189	3039	400	4193	3041	355	4198	3033	160
4190	3044	280	4194	3042	310	4199	3038	180
4191	3045	660	4195	3037	460	4200	3049	210
			4196	3048	215			
Total		1950	Total		1760	Total		710

Fig. 10.9   Production programme – work entry

Control procedures

As soon as the production plans are issued, the operations department begins the control procedures necessary to maintain an up-to-date picture of the progress of each production order. Generally, the department requires information on three stages of production:

(1)   when the cutting of a production order has to be started;
(2)   when a production order has to start being issued to the sewing room;
(3)   the styles and quantities of the finished garments which have entered the warehouse.

The department would receive the information from the sections concerned on a daily or more frequent basis. Where systems such as CIM (computerised integrated manufacturing) are employed, then the information is available in real time.

As the operations department knows the average throughput-time for each major stage of production, it can operate a control system which will generate a warning if production orders are not progressing at the correct pace. For example, if the throughput-time of the cutting room is four days, the control function would expect to see information on the cutting of a production order on the fifth day after it had been issued for cutting. The same method would be used for the making-up and finishing of garments, based on the total throughput-time of the operations involved.

For the operations department, the principle of their global control system is two questions:

(1)   Have the garments been started on time?
(2)   Have the garments been finished on time?

What goes on in between is the responsibility of production management.

Information technology

The core component of computerised planning and control systems is accurate, integrated and up-to-date information. The collection, processing and distribution of information are functions of what are called product data management (PDM) systems. These systems are communication tools that ensure that everybody in the network has access to information regarding each stage of manufacturing, from design through to deliveries to customers.

A PDM system is based on a central database, which holds general and specific 'files' for all of the subjects covered by the system. For instance, a general file could be the production programme for the next month, while a specific file could be the bill of materials for a particular garment. The files themselves are integrated so that when information is changed in one file, the related files are automatically updated. In an agile manufacturing environment, the accuracy and speed of information processing are essential tools for management.

To sum up

Although information and communication technology has reduced the time needed to plan and manage operations, accurate planning and control still rely upon the quality of the information from which scenarios are forecast and, once experienced, subsequently recorded. In an effort to reduce lead times in clothing manufacturing, planning and control need this responsivity in order to be agile and reactive to the market.

Part 3

MANUFACTURING TECHNOLOGY

11 Cutting Room

The importance of cutting

As a unit, the cutting room has a greater effect on excessive manufacturing costs than any other department concerned with the actual production of garments. These excess costs can be divided into two groups:

(1) *Internal costs*   Those incurred in the cutting room itself.
(2) *External costs*   Those incurred by other departments as a result of the malfunctions of the cutting room.

The common factors between the two groups are efficiency and quality, and each influences the other.

Internal costs

Labour

The average salary levels in the cutting room are usually the highest in the factory and to make the optimum use of expensive manpower there must be a continually balanced and controlled workflow through the cutting room. Waiting around for work or doing fill-in work is a very expensive proposition in the cutting room, apart from its effect on staff morale. The key to reducing or eliminating excess labour costs in the cutting room is once again planning and control.

Materials

Materials represents some 40–50% of the cost price of most mass-produced clothing and are the largest cost component of a garment. Excessive use of fabric caused by lack of detailed planning together with inferior spreading and cutting techniques can cause serious losses to the company. Figure 11.1 shows the factors affecting

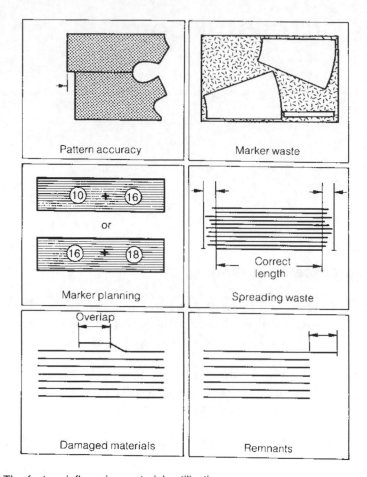

Fig. 11.1 The factors influencing materials utilisation

the use of materials and while each one has a relatively small effect, if left uncontrolled these factors can together create very serious losses.

Most of management's attention is usually directed towards saving money in the sewing room, often without realising that the savings made around the sewing machine are being squandered in the cutting room. Because the cutting room is essentially a production unit, the use of materials is very often subordinated to the demands of output and quality; this usually means that cutting production is achieved without considering the real cost to the company.

Efficiency

The fashion industry is plagued by short lead times and the cutting room has a central role to play in ensuring that garments are cut and issued for sewing in the shortest possible time. Late deliveries can lead to cancellations and the subsequent disposal of garments as 'over-production' at reduced prices. Apart from its effect on the customer confidence in the company, this type of loss can easily wipe out some or all of the hard-earned profits of the company for that particular season.

External costs

Below are some examples of how inefficiency and mistakes in the cutting room can lead to excessive costs in the sewing room.

Co-ordination

Generally a garment is made up from a number of materials such as fusibles, linings, pocketings, etc. which have to be cut, apart from the actual top cloth. The cutting room must co-ordinate its work to ensure that each batch issued to the sewing room is complete in every respect.

Having to put half-completed work aside because, say, the linings were not cut at the right time creates a stop-start situation which interferes with the production flow and obviously influences production costs.

Defects

Readily visible cloth defects must be eliminated during spreading or before issuing the work to the sewing room. There is no point in sewing a garment that will either require extensive alterations during production, or will be rejected at final inspection because of a damaged component.

Matching

Where patterned fabrics require matching during assembly, this should be possible with the minimum degree of manipulation during sewing. Apart from the extra time involved, the matching of badly aligned components would almost certainly result in distorted garments.

Accuracy

Accuracy of cutting is of supreme importance because of its influence on the correct assembly of the garment and, more importantly, on the sizing. Apart from quality problems, inaccurate cutting not only causes hold-ups in production but could also mean the costly re-cutting of components.

Sewing

Guides for sewing, such as nips, notches, drill holes, etc. must be accurate and complete. A missing guide mark might result in distorted seaming or could mean the return of the components to the cutting room for correction, which apart from the cost would also interfere with the production flow.

Shading

Where differing shades of the same colour are cut together, accurate shade marking in the cutting room is essential to prevent mixing up. The discovery of mixed shades in garments during production can create a serious problem which takes time and money to correct.

Quality

Excessive costs can be incurred by the rejection of finished garments for faults which could have been prevented in the cutting room. A realistic quality objective is to achieve the maximum number of Grade A garments from the total cut. Rejected garments are usually sold at discounted prices, resulting in a shortfall in income for the company. The same labour investment goes into a Grade A garment and a rejected garment, with the difference being in the sum received for them. Some of the major quality factors under the control of the cutting room are:

- elimination or concealment of fabric defects;
- all components cut on the correct grain lines and in accordance with the pile direction of the fabric;
- dimensionally accurate garments that do not exceed the specified tolerances;
- all materials spread at the correct tension to prevent over- or under-sized components and/or garments;
- consistent and accurate position marking.

To sum up

The importance of the cutting room in relation to the overall achievement levels of the company cannot be overstated. In fact it would be true to say that the performance level of the cutting room is the key factor in the operation of a clothing factory.

Production processes in the cutting room

Irrespective of size, all cutting rooms use the same basic system to produce cut work, with the raw materials going through the same operations in the same sequence. The factor distinguishing the operations of one cutting room from another is the level of technology employed.

Cutting production starts with the receipt of inspected raw materials, production orders and graded patterns and finishes when bundles of cut work are issued for sewing. The total process has four stages (see Fig. 11.2):

(1) planning;
(2) spreading;
(3) cutting;
(4) preparation for sewing.

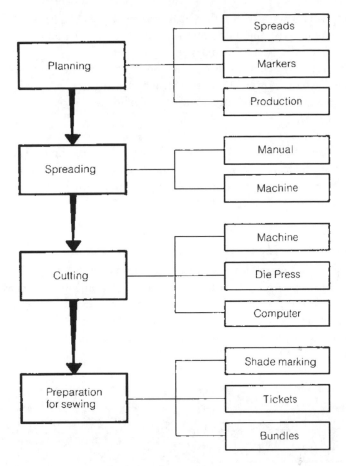

Fig. 11.2 Production processes in the cutting room

Planning

The inputs to this function are the cut order plan, which contains detailed instructions regarding the cutting markers to be planned and/or copied from existing markers, and a graded set of patterns for the style to be cut. The graded patterns can be cut out in pattern paper or may exist in the memory of a dedicated computer.

The operation itself consists of planning the layout of the pattern components so as to ensure the most economical use of materials and can be performed by one of three methods:

(1) The marker planner uses full-size patterns and arranges them in the most economical fashion on marker paper. This is a specially printed paper having symbols on it which enable the marker planner to visually control the positioning of components according to their specified grain lines.

(2) The full-size patterns are reduced, generally to a 1:5 scale, to facilitate the work of the marker planner. The miniature patterns are then arranged on a

planning board with the cloth width represented at the same scale. When the marker has been planned it is photographed, and this image is used as a guide for preparing the full-sized marker.

(3) Computerised systems are used and the marker planner works interactively with the system to plan the markers, which can then be used for manual or computer-controlled cutting. Figure 11.3 shows a screen-shot from a computerised marker planning system.

The markers can be produced on paper which is fixed to the spread with pins or staples, or on an adhesive paper which is heat-sealed to the top ply of the spread. For computerised cutting, the marker is held in position by the vacuum used to compress the spread and keep it stable.

Spreading (Fig. 11.4)

This is a preparatory operation for cutting and consists of laying plies of cloth one on top of the other in a predetermined direction and relationship between the right and wrong sides of the cloth. The composition of each spread, i.e. the number of plies of each colour, is obtained from the cut order plan.

The spreads can be of two basic types (see Fig. 11.5):

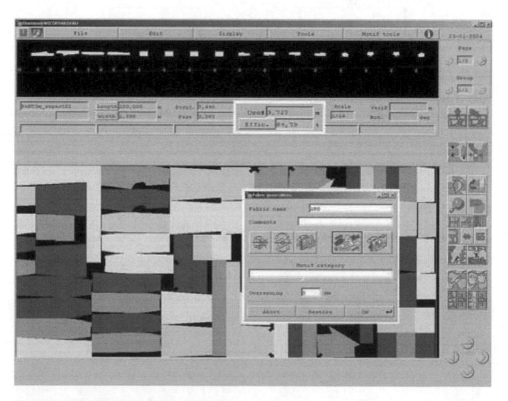

Fig. 11.3 Computerised marker planning

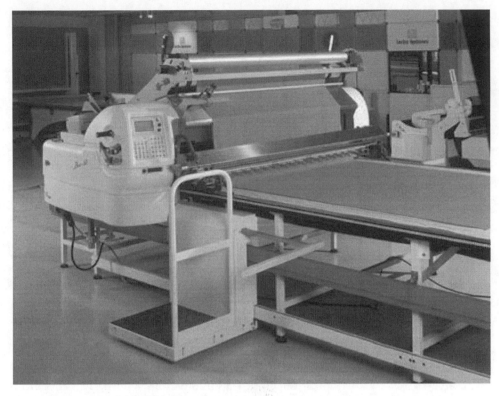

Fig. 11.4 Powered spreading machine

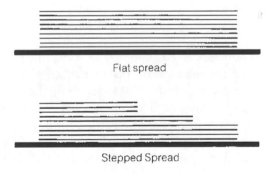

Flat spread

Stepped Spread

Fig. 11.5 Spread types

(1) *Flat spreads*   All the plies are of the same length.
(2) *Stepped spreads*   This, as the name suggests, is built up in steps, with all the plies in one step having the same length. A stepped spread is generally used when for some reason the imbalance between the quantities to be cut precludes the use of a flat spread. The cut order plan details the colours and ply lengths for a stepped spread if it is needed.

Spreading itself can be a completely manual operation or can be performed by powered machines of various levels of technology, of which some of the main features are:

- *Bolt drive* This is a mechanism which ensures that the fabric is spread with the minimum amount of tension by unwinding the fabric at exactly the same speed as the machine is moving.
- *Loading* On modern machines, this is a mechanical process whereby rolls of cloth stored in a paternoster (magazine) at the end of the table can be transferred to the machine according to a predetermined sequence or as selected by the operator.
- *Alignment* A photocell is used to sense when the alignment of the edge of a ply is starting to vary and a control motor automatically moves the roll of cloth into the correct position.
- *Ply width* Two photocells, one at each side of the machine, are indexed to the narrowest width of cloth which can be cut in the spread. If there is any deviation from the indexed width, the machine is automatically stopped and an audible signal sounded.
- *Ply counters* This device enables the machine operator to preset the number of plies to be spread, and when this number is reached the machine stops automatically.
- *Cloth roll drive* This is a cradle for holding the cloth and a group of powered conveyor belts which unroll the cloth via circumferential feed. This method is generally used for problem fabrics that require very precise control during spreading.
- *Pattern matching* An optical head is used to scan the pattern of the fabric and the sensory information is fed into a control unit which synchronises and co-ordinates the lateral and lineal movement of the cloth during spreading.
- *Programming* It is possible to programme spreading machines to perform automatically all of the major elements in the spreading process. The programme, which is prepared on the CAD system, includes cloth roll selection, loading, threading, spreading to given ply heights and lengths, etc.
- *Defect scanner* This consists of a display monitor mounted on the side of the machine, linked to the computerised marker planning system. When a cloth defect is discovered during spreading, its size and position are digitised by a projector-type cursor at the front of the spreading machine. The operator calls up the marker and the position of the defects on the marker is shown on the screen. The spreader then decides on the most appropriate course of action, without the marker having to be laid on the spread.
- *Operator comfort* Most motorised machines are equipped with a platform on which the operator can stand or sit while the machine is traversing the table.

A spreading machine is an important tool in the cutting room because it affects the efficient use of both manpower and materials.

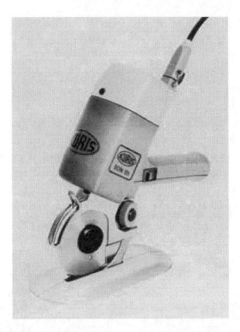

Fig. 11.6 Round knife cutting machine

Cutting

This is the major operation of the cutting room, when the spread fabric is cut into garments. Of all of the operations in the cutting room this is the most decisive, because once the fabric has been cut, very little can be done to rectify serious mistakes.

Cutting requires the use of different types of tools and some of their main features are:

- *Powered scissors* These are used for cutting one or two plies and are often used in the sample room.
- *Round knife* (Fig. 11.6) This is a very fast machine, excellent for cutting straight lines or gradual curves. Blade sizes range from 4 cm to 20 cm in diameter and the effective cutting height is about 40% of the blade diameter.
- *Straight knife* (Fig. 11.7) The workhorse of most cutting rooms, the straight knife, if correctly used, is versatile and accurate enough for most purposes.
- *Band knife* (Fig. 11.8) The narrow blade of this machine allows the finest of shapes to be cut very accurately. Some band knife machines have air flotation tables which support the block of work on a fine air cushion, enabling the cutter to manoeuvre the work during cutting with the minimum disturbance to the plies.
- *Servo-assisted cutting* (Fig. 11.9) This consists of a straight knife cutting machine on an articulated arm at the side of the cutting table. The system has a servo-drive which enables the cutting machine to be moved easily in all directions while maintaining the right angle between the blade and the table.

- *Press cutting*   (Fig. 11.10) This process involves the use of a hydraulic press which forces a shaped metal cutting die through a pile of material and is mostly used when large quantities of small components have to be cut very accurately. Press cutting is also often used for cutting many of the components for leather and suede garments.
- *Computer-controlled cutting*   (Fig. 11.11) The input for this operation comes from the markers generated on computerised marker planning systems. The marker data is transferred to the cutting unit by means of tapes, floppy disks or streamers or directly from the marker planning system itself. Computerised cutting is six to eight times faster than any manual method and produces cut components with a consistent level of accuracy. Although a computerised cutting system requires a substantial initial investment, it is considered to be the most effective investment for large-scale cutting production. Less expensive systems are available for factories having smaller quantities to cut and these systems also pay their way.

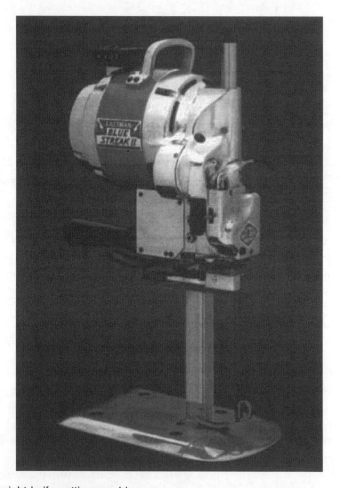

Fig. 11.7   Straight knife cutting machine

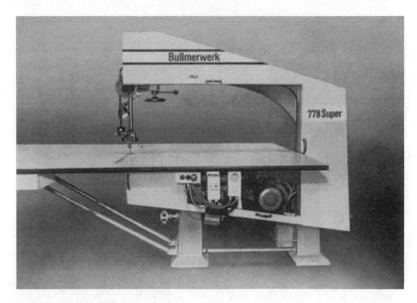

Fig. 11.8   Band knife cutting machine

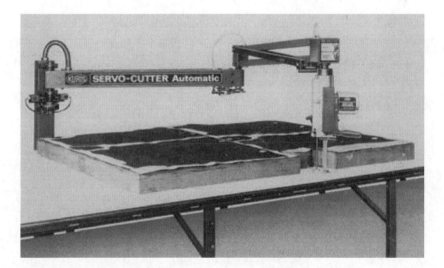

Fig. 11.9   Servo-assisted cutting system

Preparation for sewing

The next group of operations are concerned with preparing the cut components for sewing, and include the following.

Position marking

When required, this operation marks components with guides for sewing and other operations. Figure 11.12 shows a drill marker used for marking pocket positions,

Fig. 11.10 Hydraulic swing arm press

Fig. 11.11 Computer-controlled cuting system

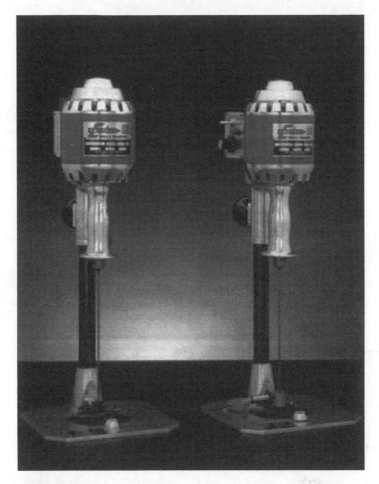

Fig. 11.12 Drill marker

dart lengths, etc. The mark itself can be a very small hole or a mark made by a chalk-based liquid taken through the spread by the drill flutes.

Shade marking

This operation ensures that components cut from different shades of the same colour do not get mixed up during the assembly process. Every component for one garment is marked with a unique number, usually printed on a small ticket (Fig. 11.13) which is stuck on the component.

Bundle preparation

Bundles of cut work are prepared according to size, colour and quantities, their actual composition determined by the requirements of the sewing room. For example, all the components for one bundle of garments can be packed into one

Fig. 11.13   Tickets produced on a shade marking machine

Order no. 6014	Bundle 1480	Quan. 22	Op. S34
	Operator		
Bundle no. 1480	Bundle 1480	Quan. 22	Op. S31
	Operator		
Quantity 22	Bundle 1480	Quan. 22	Op. S29
Style no. 3642	Operator		
Size 16			
	Bundle 1480	Quan. 22	Op S28
Section Sleeves	Operator	652	

Remains with bundle   For operator and control

Fig. 11.14   Bundle ticket

box, or each of the major components packed in its own container ready to be issued to different preparation and sub-assembly sections in the factory. Alternatively, if unit production systems (see Chapter 15) are used, the components for single garments can be loaded directly into the system from the cutting table.

Bundle tickets

These tickets identify each bundle and in themselves play an important role in production planning and control for the sewing and finishing sections. The tickets themselves can be in alphanumeric form (Fig. 11.14) or bar-coded, and in both cases they can be computer generated.

To sum up

The cutting room holds many of the keys essential to the performance and quality levels of the factory. All things considered, an efficient cutting room is the best foundation a production unit can have.

12 Fusing Technology

The term fusible interlining is applied to a base fabric having a deposit of thermoplastic resin (usually on one side only) which can be bonded to another fabric by heat and pressure. In total, fusing technology is concerned with:

- base cloths;
- resins;
- coating systems;
- machinery and equipment;
- control of quality.

Base cloths

The base cloth, also called the substrate, is an interlining material on which the thermoplastic resin is coated, sprayed or printed. Base cloths are produced in a variety of woven, knitted and non-woven forms from natural or synthetic fibres and each type has a specific application.

Irrespective of the construction and fibres used, the base cloth influences the following characteristics in the finished garment:

- handle and bulk;
- shape retention;
- shrinkage control;
- crease recovery;
- appearance in wear;
- appearance after dry-cleaning or washing;
- durability.

In addition, the final cost of the garment is influenced by the type and amount of fusibles used in its construction.

Resins

These are the materials applied to the base cloth, and when subjected to heat and pressure they become the sole bonding agent between the top cloth and the inter-lining. Thermoplasticity, or change with heat, is the basis of all fusible interlinings; in its cold state the resin is not adhesive and only becomes viscous when heated. Through the application of pressure, the heated resin penetrates into the top cloth; on cooling it solidifies again, forming a bond between the two fabrics.

Today no naturally occurring resins are used for interlinings, but a large variety of thermoplastic resins including polyamides, polyester and PVC.

Coating systems

Coating is the process whereby the thermoplastic resin is applied to the substrate material. There are many coating methods in use, some of the more commonly used ones being:

- *Scatter coating* This method uses electronically controlled scattering heads to deposit the resin on to the moving substrate.
- *Dry-dot printing* In this process, the resin is printed on to the substrate by a roller engraved with small indentations which hold the resin powder.
- *Preformed* The resin is heat-processed to form a net which is then laminated on to the base cloth by heat and pressure. During heating, the net melts and leaves a minute dot pattern on the substrate.

A coating system is basically concerned with flexibility and uniformity, and these factors have to be considered when evaluating the use of specific fusibles.

Machinery and equipment

The mechanical medium required for fusing is a press, and the three basic types are:

(1) steam;
(2) flat bed;
(3) continuous-fusing.

Steam press

Regular steam presses with shaped bucks are not designed for fusing but are used for this purpose by many factories who cannot, or will not, invest in the correct equipment. While fusibles with certain types of resin can be fused on steam presses, these machines have a number of serious limitations for general use, including the following:

- Even when fitted with heated bucks, steam presses are usually unable to reach the heat levels required by most resins.
- The pressure applied over the full buck area is uneven, which restricts the machine's use to the fusing of small parts.
- Most of the older type of steam presses are not fitted with timers and programme controls, thus leaving the time element completely dependent on the operator.
- When the resin has been originally activated by steam heat, the same thing can happen again when garments are pressed during production. This is likely to cause serious problems with lamination and handling.

All in all, steam presses do not have the complete range of operating characteristics necessary for correct fusing.

Flat bed press

These are purpose-built fusing machines available in a wide variety of types from small table models to large, floor-standing machines. There is also a wide choice of manual or mechanical loading and take-off systems for use with these presses.

Basically this type of press consists of padded top and bottom bucks with heating elements in one or both of the bucks. The bottom buck is static, with the top buck raised or lowered to open or close the press. Flat bed presses can have single or double trays which move horizontally to feed work into and extract it from the machine. There are many types of special-purpose flat bed presses which are built to suit a particular, repetitive type of operation. One of these (Fig. 12.1) has a

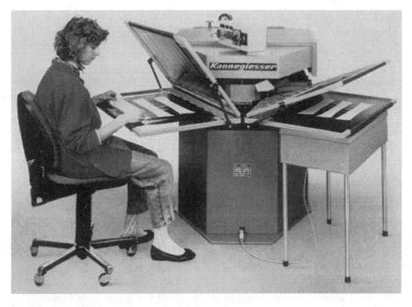

Fig. 12.1 Carousel fusing press

Fig. 12.2 Conveyor fusing press

carousel action which automatically moves the assembly from the loading position of the operator through the fusing and cooling processes and returns the fused components to the operator for unloading.

There are a large range of flat-bed presses available for different purposes, which enables a factory to equip itself with the right machines for each job.

Continuous-fusing press (Fig. 12.2)

These machines all operate on the same principle, transporting the assembly for fusing through all the processes on a powered conveyor belt. There are two conveyor belt systems in general use:

- *End-to-end feed* The parts are conveyed from the loading area at one end of the machine, via the fusing and cooling areas, to the take-off area at the opposite end of the machine. This system is used where production levels require one set of operators for loading and another set for unloading.
- *Return feed* This machine has a belt system which returns the fused components to the same end of the machine at which they were loaded. The upper belt transports the unit through the fusing processes and the lower belt returns the fused unit to its starting point. This enables the operators to load and unload from the same position.

Continuous fusing presses are also available for special purposes such as the fusing of trouser and skirt waistbands or other narrow components which can be fused in continuous tape form.

Fusing is known to be a labour-intensive operation and in the past few years there have been some major developments which substantially reduce the manual labour content. Two examples of these developments are:

- *Modular stacker* This apparatus is positioned at the exit end of the continuous press and has four modules, the operating area of each one equal to one-quarter of the conveyor belt width. Each conveyor lane, or combination of lanes, is allocated to the fusing of one specific component. The stacker works independently of the conveyor belt speed and is activated by photocells which can sense the position of the component. Work is removed from the belt by a simple grasping mechanism and automatically stacked in bundle form on a rack. When the bundle has been completed it is removed by the operator, so cutting out most of the handling required by the unloading and stacking of single components.
- *Robotics* A development in automation for the loading area is a robotic system which picks up and positions the fusible on to the top cloth. The operator places the cloth component on to the conveyor belt and the visual capability of the robot enables it to locate the correct position for the fusible while the cloth component is being transported past the work station. The robotic systems available are only capable of picking up and positioning relatively small components. The limp and flexible nature of textile materials has proven to be a serious limitation to the development of robotic systems.

A concerted research effort has been directed towards finding alternative and more efficient methods of fusing. One method used a high-frequency system to melt the resin, while another method printed the stabilisation material directly on to the top cloth. Neither of these methods were found to be commercially viable, but while both have been discontinued, it does not mean that the last has been heard of these innovative developments.

The control of quality

Relatively speaking, fusible interlinings are precision products and it is essential that they are fused on the correct equipment and under strict control. Some factors which influence fusing quality are:

(1) temperature;
(2) time;
(3) pressure;
(4) peel-strength;
(5) dry-clean and/or wash.

Temperature

There is a limited range of temperatures effective for each resin. The applied heat generated by the machine can be checked by a simple and practical method involving the use of thermal test papers. These are narrow strips of paper calibrated in increments of 2°C, which react to temperature by changing the colour of the segment with the matching temperature rating.

Time

The only time element of any value in fusing is when the assemblies are actually being heated. For flat bed presses this is the time between the closing and opening of the bucks; for continuous machines it is the time when the assemblies are actually in the heating zones of the machine.

Generally, a flat bed press has a mechanical timer which can be verified by a stopwatch. The time element for a continuous machine is checked by measuring the conveyor belt speed with a tachometer.

Pressure

During fusing it is necessary to apply equal pressure all over the component in order to ensure that:

- an intimate contact is effected between the top cloth and the interlining;
- the heat transfer is optimum;
- there is a controlled and even penetration of the resin points into the fibres of the top cloth.

There are many methods of verifying whether pressure is being exerted equally over the pressure surfaces of the machine. One of the simplest is to fuse a large piece of cloth with an identically sized piece of fusible. After cooling, the fused assembly should be carefully separated. In some cases the interlining fibres will remain on the cloth and in others the fibres of the cloth will be pulled out by the fusible. In both cases, a clear optical pattern will result which would indicate the areas where there are pressure variations. Serious variations of adhesion need the attention of skilled technicians.

Peel-strength test

This test checks the strength of the bond between the top cloth and the interlining; the force required to pull them apart is compared to a standard for that particular cloth and fusible. The test is usually performed on a fused strip about 70 cm × 5 cm with the length on the warp of the cloth. The force required to separate them can be measured on an instrument called a tensometer, or more simply with a good spring balance.

Dry-clean and/or wash

It is recommended that production garments should be subjected to the appropriate cleaning methods on a regular basis. One garment in each cloth and fusible combination should be tested at least once every two working weeks.

To sum up

Fusing is an integral part of clothing manufacture and there is no doubt that garment quality and durability are inexorably bound to the overall effectiveness of this process.

13 Sewing Technology

The components of sewing

The central process in the manufacture of clothing is the joining together of multiple 2-D fabric pieces to form a 3-D garment – operations that all involve sewing in one form or another. Although there are a large number of different categories of sewing machine, their actual sewing functions are all derived from the same component parts of sewing. A brief examinations of these follows, then other aspects of machinery and equipment are discussed.

Stitches

Stitch formation consists of one or more thread supplies being combined together to form a stitch. These are defined as:

- *Intralooping* The passing of one loop of thread through another loop of the same thread supply; an example of this is 101 single thread chainstitch.
- *Interlooping* The passing of a thread through a loop formed by a separate thread supply; an example of this is a 401 two thread chainstitch.
- *Interlacing* The passing of a thread around, or over, a separate thread supply or a loop of that supply; an example of this is a 301 two thread lockstitch.

Every category of sewing machine produces a specific type of stitch formation depending on the number of needles, loop taking mechanisms and threads which combine to construct the stitch. Each of these configurations is known as a stitch type and they are classified according to their main characteristics. There are various national and international standards for stitch types and they all use a similar taxonomy for classifying the main and sub-classes of stitch types. The following is an example of the system used by the British and USA standards, both of which contain the specifications for over 70 different stitch types. The six main classes are identified by the first of the three digits:

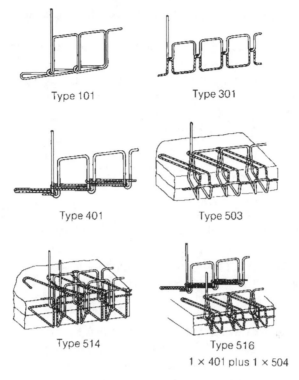

Type 101   Type 301

Type 401   Type 503

Type 514   Type 516
                  1 × 401 plus 1 × 504

Fig. 13.1   Common stitch types

Class 100:   chain-type stitches
Class 200:   hand-formed stitches
Class 300:   lock stitches
Class 400:   locked chainstitches
Class 500:   over-edging stitches
Class 600:   flat seam or covering stitches

The applications of some of the sub-classes are described here and the stitch constructions are shown in Figure 13.1.

Sub-class 101

Chainstitches are formed by the intralooping of a needle thread supply on or around the fabric. They are often used for temporary applications as they are easy to remove. This is because each successive loop is dependent upon the previous loop for security.

Applications of this stitch type are:

- *Basting* Temporary holding of fabric pieces before final securing stitch is introduced.

- *Sack Closure* Ease of removal allows use for securing industrial sacking openings.
- *Coinelli* Up to 65 needles can be employed to produce decorative seams with the chain on the face fabric.
- *Button sew and button-holing* The single thread gives lightweight but secure fixing for buttons and a clean finish to the mouth of a button hole.

The end of seam must be secured in all cases to prevent the stitches from unravelling.

Sub-class 301

This is the most widely used of all stitch types and is the stitch produced by a regular sewing machine. It is also the easiest stitch to identify as it is the only stitch formation to have the same appearance on both sides of the seam. This stitch is formed by interlacing a needle thread supply with the spool thread supply underneath. The stitches are very secure as a break in one stitch will not cause the seam to completely unravel although it will compromise the overall seam performance.

Another advantage of using this stitch is that it is the only stitch to reliably sew round 90° when pivoting the fabric at the needle point. This is very useful when sewing items such as labels and badges. It is also very important when stitching collars and cuffs where precise stitching is required. A disadvantage of using this stitch is that spool thread changes are frequently required, thus reducing the productive capacity of the machine.

Sub-class 401

This stitch is formed by the interlooping of a needle thread with a separate looper thread on the underside of the fabric. It is often referred to as a double-locked stitch because each needle thread loop is interconnected with two loops of the same single underthread. It has the appearance of a lock-stitch (301) on the top surface with a double chain underneath.

The stitch exhibits good strength and increased extension/recovery properties as a result of lower static thread tensions and interlooped threads which gives it greater elasticity. It is less prone to seam pucker, for the same reasons. This stitch is excellent for long seams because of continuous thread supplies.

Sub-class 503

This two-thread overlock stitch is sometimes used as a cheaper alternative to the regular three-thread overlock stitch sub-class 504 (Fig. 13.2), which is the most common stitch usually found on an overlocking machine.

Many variations of overlock (500 class) stitch exist employing from one to four threads. They are generally used to neaten the cut edge of the fabric plies. The needle thread provides the seam strength while the looper threads provide the cover

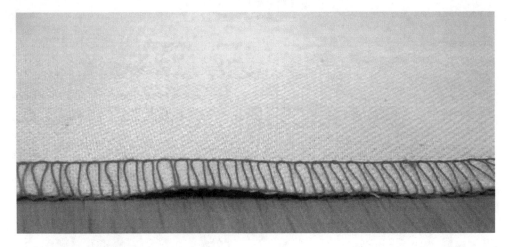

Fig. 13.2 Stitch type 504

on the edge of the material. The sewing threads in the loopers are chosen for their softness and appearance.

Sub-class 514

This stitch is constructed from four threads, employing two needle threads and two looper threads. This stitch formation is used to join and neaten seams where there is no necessity to press open the seam. The inside needle thread is commonly known as a mock safety stitch and is so called because only one side of the needle thread can be seen clearly; the other side is hidden in the stitch. It is used to provide strength to the seam whilst reducing seam bulkiness.

This type of stitch formation is used in the manufacture of T-shirts, shirts, blouses and many other operations where extra strength is required without increasing the unwieldiness of the seam. An example can be seen in Figure 13.3.

Sub-class 516

This stitch, known as a safety stitch (or more commonly, a combination stitch), combines sub-class 401, a two-thread locked chain stitch, with sub-class 504, which is the regular three-thread overlock stitch. The sewing action is to overlock and join the plies simultaneously. The seam can be pressed or top-stitched to one side. The main reasons for using this stitch are for its strength and its durability. The overlocking stitch provides the neatening on the edge of the seam and the two-thread stitch type 401 provides the strength.

This type of stitch is used in the manufacture of denim jeans and for other types of medium- to heavy-weight materials.

Sub-class 605

This is a cover stitch that uses three needles, one looper and a spreader that spreads a top thread over the top of the material. Advantages of these machines are that

Fig. 13.3   514 overlocking stitch with mock safety stitch

they have very good extension properties; they are commonly used in underwear, skiwear and various forms of knitwear. Also in some cases they eliminate some overlocking operations as they can join raw edges of fabric together while still maintaining good fabric cover. An example of a cover stitch is given in Figure 13.4.

Seams

A seam is a joint where a sequence of stitches unite two or more pieces of material. Seams, like stitches, are classified according to main and sub-classes. The main classes according to the British and USA standards are:

British standard	Federal standard	Description	Example
Class 1	SS	Superimposed	SSa-1
Class 2	LS	Lapped	LSc-1
Class 3	BS	Bound	BSa-1
Class 4	FS	Flat	Efa-1

Representative examples of these seam types are shown in Figure 13.5.

When choosing a seam for a garment operation, the following factors should be considered:

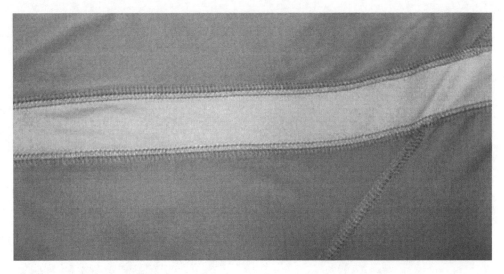

Fig. 13.4 Cover stitch 605

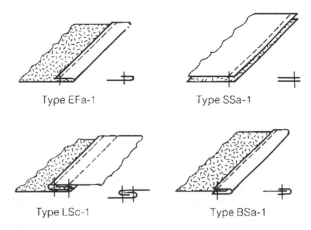

Fig. 13.5   Seam types

- aesthetic appeal;
- strength;
- durability;
- comfort in wear;
- ease of assembly;
- equipment availability;
- cost.

A seam should be suitable for the purpose for which it is intended and seam type is dependent upon the product being sewn. It must combine the required standards of appearance and performance while ensuring economy of production.

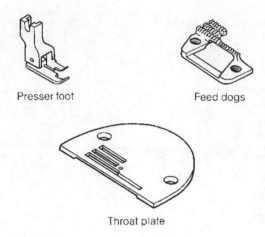

Fig. 13.6 Feed system components

Feed systems

This is the term used to describe the components and mechanisms which feed the work through the machine to enable a series of stitches to be formed. The constituent parts of a feed system are as follows (see Fig. 13.6).

Presser foot

The foot is used to hold the material against the throat plate and prevent it from moving out of alignment with the needle and feed dog movement.

Throat plate

This provides a smooth surface for the material to pass over, and has one or more slots to accommodate the movement of the feed dogs. The throat plate also has a needle hole(s) and sometimes a slot for sewing needle actions such as that of a zigzag machine.

Feed dogs

These move the material forward a predetermined distance to allow successive penetrations of the needle. The stitch regulator fitted to machines controls the distance the work travels between each penetration, and this distance is called stitch length.

Some examples of the various feed systems in common use are shown in Figures 13.7 to 13.11, with the movement during forward sewing of the feed dogs, top feeds and needles shown by dotted lines and arrows.

Needles

These were probably among the first tools devised by man to still remain in use today. The first needles had a split head for grasping the sinews, fibres or

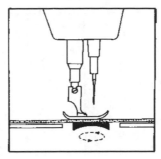

Fig. 13.7   Drop feed: This feed system is used on all regular sewing machines for flat seams on materials where inter-ply shifting is unlikely to occur

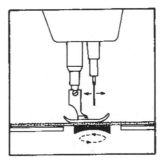

Fig. 13.8   Compound feed: The combined needle and feed dog movement ensures that plies do not shift out of alignment while being sewn. A feed of this type is used for sewing a slippery material such as velvet, or for top-stitching edges

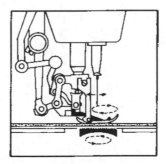

Fig. 13.9   Unison feed: This features the synchronised movement of the needle, feed dogs and top feed with the foot. This feed system is especially suitable for operations where several plies of material have to be joined, for example when sandwiching a finished collar between the body and the neck line facing

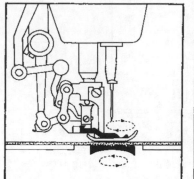
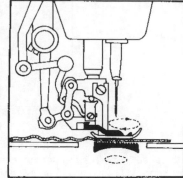

Fig. 13.10 Drop and variable top feed: The top and bottom feeds can be adjusted to create fullness on the top ply by means of a stretching action on the lower ply. A typical operation using this feed is the closing of shoulder seams

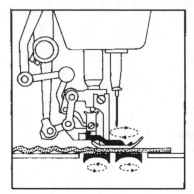
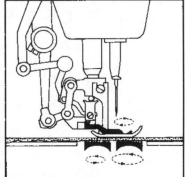

Fig. 13.11 Differential bottom and variable top feed: The action of this feed system is capable of very fine adjustments between the top and bottom feeds and is used on slippery fabrics where fullness has to be created on the top or bottom plies. One example would be the slight easing of a satin lining on to the facing of a velvet garment

leather strips while they were being drawn through the materials. Needles with eyes emerged about 17500 BC and around AD 1800 the eye of the needle was moved from the head to near the point, which paved the way for sewing development.

The construction features and terminology for a basic sewing machine needle are shown in Figure 13.12. Some of the more important factors regarding needles are:

(1) *Shape* (Fig. 13.13) This refers to the shape of the blade, which is the central length section of the needle and can be straight or curved depending on the sewing action of the machine. For example, a regular sewing machine uses a vertically moving straight needle, while a blind-stitch machine with a horizontal type of sewing action requires a curved needle.

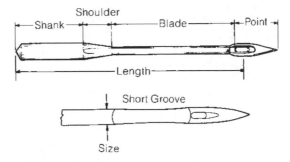

Fig. 13.12 The construction of a needle

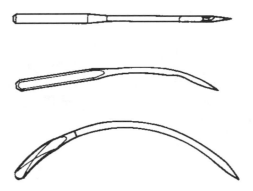

Fig. 13.13 Needle shapes

(2) *Length*   For most needles the length is measured from the top of the shank to the centre of the eye. The shank is the upper end of the needle which fits into the needle bar.

(3) *Size*   This refers to the diameter of the blade above the eye or short groove clearance. For cylindrical needle blades, the metric size (Nm) equals the blade diameter multiplied by 100. Because many different nomenclatures are used to describe the size of needles, it is common to find the equivalents between systems shown in the manufacturer's handbook which comes with the sewing machine.

(4) *Eye*   The most frequently used shape is like a rectangle with semicircular ends, and the width of the eye is usually about 40 per cent of the blade diameter. Eyes larger than this are used when sewing with knopped or embroidery-type threads.

(5) *Point*   The most important aspect of needle design is the point (Fig. 13.14) because it has to penetrate the fabric without cutting or causing other damage. As a rule, fine round point needles are used for delicate fabrics while sturdier round points are preferable for coarser cloths. Stub points are very suitable for sewing buttons, hooks, etc., because the shape of the point is strong enough to centralise holes which are slightly out of alignment.

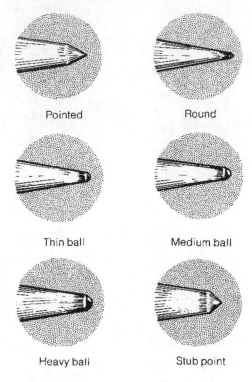

Pointed   Round

Thin ball   Medium ball

Heavy ball   Stub point

Fig. 13.14   Needle points for woven and knitted fabrics

Threads

Sewing threads are made from natural or synthetic fibres or a blend of both and they are chosen according to their suitability for sewing in relation to:

- *Uniform thickness*   This permits the easy, rapid movement of thread, when under tension, through the needle's eye and the fabric.
- *Smoothness*   Essential if the thread is to withstand the friction of high-speed sewing.
- *Elasticity*   The thread must make supple stitches which will not pucker or break under seam strain.
- *Strength*   To hold seams secure during the reasonable life of a garment.

Most sewing threads start as simple yarns produced by twisting together relatively short fibres or fine continuous filaments. The twist inserted into these basic yarns provides the consolidating force and this is balanced by applying a reverse twist when two or more yarns are combined to form a thread. Without this reverse twist, the individual plies of a conventional thread would separate during their continuous movement through the needle and other friction points in the sewing mechanism. Twist can be applied in a clockwise (Z twist) or anticlockwise (S twist) direction (see Fig. 13.15a).

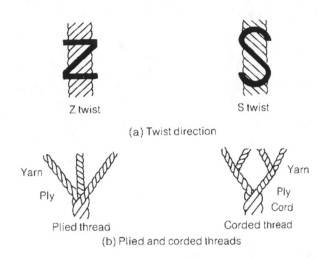

Fig. 13.15   Sewing thread construction

The object of these twists is to negate the actions of sewing machines which tend to unwind the thread. During sewing a regular sewing machine introduces a slight Z twist in the thread; this is offset by using a Z twist thread that has sufficient slack in its construction to allow it to be slightly tightened. Against this, an S twist thread would become untwisted and then fray and break. The majority of sewing machines use Z twist threads; S twists are only used when the stitching action of the machine demands it.

Sewing threads are mainly produced in two or three plies, and these plied threads are used when a finer thread is required. Heavier, or corded, threads are made by combining plied threads. Both these thread types are illustrated in Figure 13.15b.

The size of a sewing thread is designated by a number known as its yarn count, grist or size. The sizing systems used are mainly based on a fixed weight or length. Three of the most universally used systems are fixed weight, fixed length and ticket number.

Fixed weight

These systems show the length or number of length units which make up a given weight of yarn. For example, the cotton count indicates how many hanks 840 yards long weigh one pound, starting at a count 1 cotton thread where one hank weighs one pound.

Fixed length

This method of sizing is called the Tex or Decitex System. The count number is equivalent to the weight in grams of 10 000 metres. If, for example, a yarn has a Decitex count of 180 this means that 10 000 metres of this yarn weigh 180 grams, and if two of these yarns were twisted into one thread the count number would be 360.

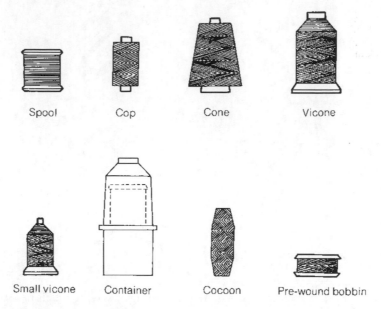

Fig. 13.16   Sewing thread packages

Ticket number

This widely used system is based on the cotton and metric count systems where the ticket numbers are approximately equal to three times the original count. In both the cotton and metric systems, the count number is inversely proportional to the size or weight per unit length of the thread. So a ticket number 20 thread is twice as coarse as a ticket number 40 thread.

Sewing threads come packaged in various sizes which provide for short- or long-term use of the same thread and colour. Figure 13.16 shows some of the most frequently used types of packaging.

To sum up

There are many variants in the components of sewing and it is only when they are accurately balanced with each other that sewing can be performed efficiently and at a consistent standard of quality.

Machinery and equipment

It has been estimated that there are over 3000 different types of sewing machine on the market. This is not surprising in view of the number of products which incorporate sewing in their manufacture. Apart from all types of clothing, there are tents, curtains, bedlinen, upholstery, shoes, luggage, parachutes, etc., all of which contain sewn elements.

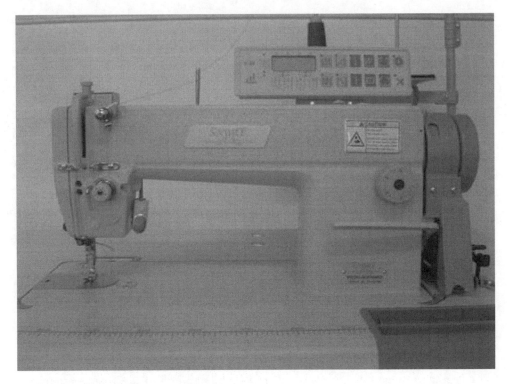

Fig. 13.17   Regular sewing machine

For the clothing industry there is a great diversity of regular and special machines for sewing every conceivable type of garment and it is this variety which enables clothing manufacturers to employ specialised equipment for their own particular requirements. While there is a vast range, some machines are basic items of equipment in nearly every sewing room, and brief descriptions of these follow.

Basic sewing machines

General sewing (Fig. 13.17)

The single-needle lock-stitch machine has evolved considerably over the past few decades. Some of the features of the machines in common use today are:

- speeds of up to 6000 rpm with electronic controls which reduce the time required for acceleration and deceleration;
- automatic positioning of the needle in an up or down position;
- the automatic cutting of top and bottom threads;
- a back-tacking mechanism actuated through the foot pedal or automatically by means of an electronic seam-end sensor;
- automatic foot-lifting actuated by the foot pedal instead of a manual knee lift;
- programmable sewing sequences via a microprocessor for repetitive operations.

Fig. 13.18 Overlock machine with puller feed useful for sewing long seams, slippery fabrics, etc.

The regular sewing machine is often regarded as an end in itself rather than as a basic sewing tool. However, there are an enormous variety of feed types, attachments and apparatus available to make this machine into one of the most versatile items of equipment in the sewing room.

Overlocking (Fig. 13.18)

This is the generic name given to over-edge stitch machines used to trim and cover the rough edges of the fabric in order to present a clean and neat appearance where seam edges are visible. Overlock machines are also used for the assembly of some types of knitted articles such as T-shirts.

The over-edge stitch can be formed from one to four threads. Some of the technological highlights of these machines are:

- speeds of up to 10 000 rpm;
- automatic thread-cutting;
- a vacuum system for extracting cloth waste and thread ends;
- variable feeds for sewing problem materials;
- creating continuous or intermittent fullness on the top or bottom when joining two plies.

Safety-stitching

Safety stitch machines have the same features as overlock machines and are used for the simultaneous seaming and overlocking of many garments where there is

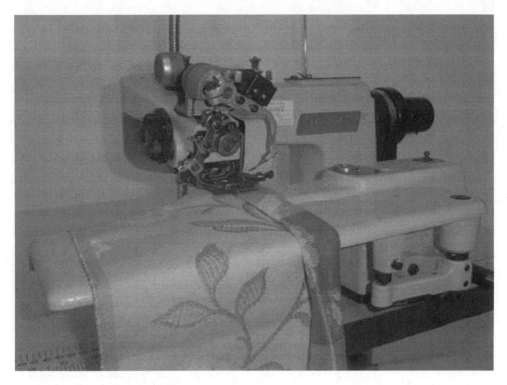

Fig. 13.19 Blind stitch machine

no necessity for pressed-open seams. There are two types of safety stitch machines in general use, the main difference between them being the number of threads used to construct the stitching, which consists of a locked chainstitch parallel to an over-locked edge.

With the four-thread machine, one of the looper threads of the overlock stitch is used as the bottom thread for the chainstitch. On a five-thread machine, each row of stitches has its own threads, i.e. three for the overlock and two for the chainstitch.

Blind stitching (Fig. 13.19)

These machines are used for fastening hems or facings and, as the name suggests, they perform this operation without the stitch impression showing on the right side of the garment. This class of machine uses a curved needle which is designed to slightly penetrate the surface of the fabric but emerges on the same side as it entered.

Most blind stitch machines are fitted with an optional skipstitch device which causes the machine to catch the outside layer every second or third stitch while catching the inside layer with every stitch. This device is very important for the hemming of fine fabrics. Some features of blind stitch machines are:

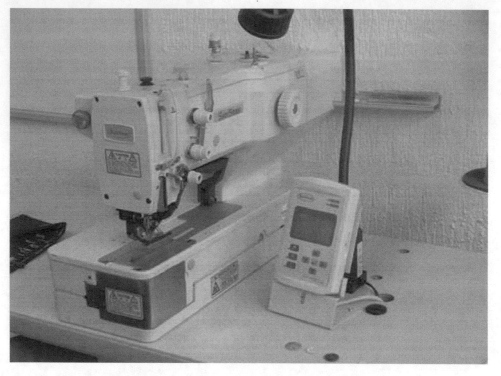

Fig. 13.20   Electronic, programmable buttonhole machine

- sewing speeds of up to 2000 st/min;
- automatic thread clipping;
- automatic needle positioning;
- pneumatic opening and closing of the work plate;
- one- or two-thread versions, and with the two-thread machine the stitch is locked in order to prevent it unravelling.

The machine illustrated is a single-thread version which is used for hemming heavy fabrics.

Buttonholes (Fig. 13.20)

A buttonhole is a straight or shaped slit cut through the garment and then sewn round its edges to prevent fraying and stretching. The cut shape of the buttonhole and the number of threads used to cover its edges depend on the garment type and quality. For example, the buttonholes in a man's jacket would be strongly constructed to withstand frequent opening and closing, whereas the buttonholes for a woman's blouse would have a lighter construction because they are used far less during wear. On non-fray fabrics the buttonhole is cut before sewing, but with fabrics which have a marked tendency to fray the sewing is performed before the cutting. The advance of electronic and microprocessing technology has also made

Fig. 13.21 Bartack machine

it possible for buttonhole machines to be programmed to do different lengths and shapes of buttonholes, enabling greater flexibility and efficiency.

Where standard types of garments, such as shirts, are being produced, the buttonholes are automatically sewn and spaced at predetermined distances. The operator simply positions the work in the machine and starts the cycle. An unloading device removes and stacks the sewn work after completion of the cycle, thus enabling the operator to work on more than one buttonholing unit.

Bartacking (Fig. 13.21)

The bartack machine has many applications in the clothing industry; one of them is the sewing of a dense tack across the open end of a buttonhole. The machine sews a number of stitches across the end of the buttonhole, then oversews them at right angles with a series of covering stitches. Each machine sews a fixed number of stitches with the option to change stitch density, and machines are available which sew bartacks containing from 18 to 42 stitches.

The illustration shows a machine used for bartacking the belt loops of trousers and some of these types of machine are fitted with:

- a mechanism which signals audibly and visually when the spool thread is below a certain level;
- automatic thread-cutting at the end of the sewing cycle;
- a two-stage pedal which opens and closes the work clamp and also operates the machine;
- a brake wheelbase which enables the machine to be easily moved.

In other specialised versions, bartack machines are used for sewing small decorative tacks and shapes.

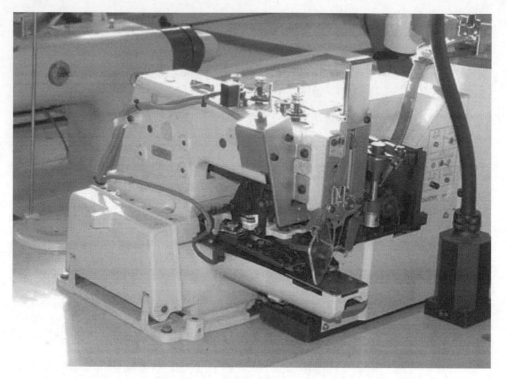

Fig. 13.22   Electronic button sewing machine with automatic button feeding

Button sewing (Fig. 13.22)

Buttons with two holes, four holes or shanks can all be sewn on the same machine by simple adjustments to the button clamp and the spacing mechanism. The sewing action consists of a series of parallel stitches whose length is equal to the spacing between the centres of the holes. The needle has a vertical movement only and the button is moved from side to side by the button clamp.

Buttons can be sewn on with one or two threads, the number of stitches depending on the type of machine used. Each machine has a maximum number of stitches, i.e. 16, 24 or 32, and can be adjusted to sew the full amount or half, i.e. 8 or 16, 12 or 24, and 16 or 32. Generally, decorative buttons would be sewn on with half the number of stitches used for functional buttons. Where a 'neck' is required between the under side of the button and the garment, the stitch length between the button and the garment is increased and this surplus length can be left as it is, or 'whipped'. The whipping operation can be performed as a separate operation after button sewing, or can be incorporated as a second, successive operation on the button-sewing machine.

Special sewing machines

Apart from the basic general-purpose sewing machines, there is also a huge range of high-performance special machines that are built to perform one operation only

Fig. 13.23 Automatic seaming machines can be used for long seaming operations, trouser legs, curtains, etc

at a consistently high level of quality. The concept behind these machines is to reduce the skills input of the operator and build them into the machine instead. Ideally the operator is required only to feed the machine rather than control the operation, and this type of sewing machine technology is becoming more and more common in every sector of the clothing industry. An example of this is an automatic seaming machine (Figure 13.23).

To sum up

The evaluation and selection of sewing machinery can sometimes be difficult and confusing because of the choice available for nearly every type of machine. This is aggravated when there is very little difference in price and performance between the machines.

A point to consider: purchasing a sewing machine is not just a commercial transaction but means that the purchaser is getting involved with another small but long-term partner – the supplier. In the final analysis, it is the supplier's integrity and reputation for advice, service, training and spares that really counts in the long run.

Work aids

Although the term work aids generally refers to apparatus fitted on to sewing machines, the subject itself is far more extensive. All work aids, irrespective of type, have the same primary objective: to increase the time the operator spends sewing.

It is a well-established fact in the clothing industry that the average sewing machine is actually stitching for about 20–25% of the operator's working time. The rest of the time is taken up with arranging, handling and disposing of work in addition to bobbin changes, rethreading, etc. and attending to personal needs. Consequently any device which helps increase sewing time automatically increases the operator's output.

So in the wider sense, work aids also include the items described in this section.

Machine beds

These are made in different standard shapes and each type is built to allow for the easy movement of the type of components sewn on the machine. A bed which is not appropriate for the part being sewn just makes the operator's work more tedious and time-consuming. Figure 13.24 shows the four basic types of machine bed, together with a description of their usual applications.

Another possible variation is in the mounting of the machine to the machine table and this particularly applies to over-edge machines such as overlockers or

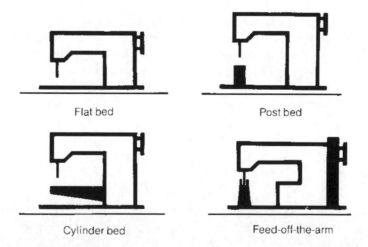

Flat bed   Post bed

Cylinder bed   Feed-off-the-arm

Fig. 13.24 Sewing machine beds. Flat bed: The most widely used type of machine bed for flat sewing. Cylinder bed: The shape of this bed allows for the easy rotation of tubular parts, such as the cuff of an assembled sleeve during a felling operation. Post bed: The upright arm has a relatively small sewing area and this, combined with its height, allows for a part to be grasped and turned without difficulty. A typical operation for this bed shape is sleeve setting. Feed-off-the-arm: Built expressly for closing cylindrical parts, this bed shape is used for lap-seaming the outside leg seams of trousers after the inside leg seam has been closed.

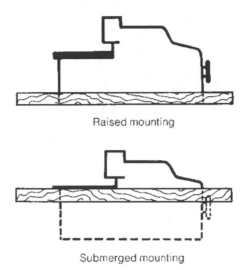

Raised mounting

Submerged mounting

Fig. 13.25 Overlock machine mountings

safety stitch machines. Figure 13.25 shows the alternative mountings: in the raised position the plate is above the table surface, while the submerged position presents a flat sewing surface with the table.

Machine tables

These are built in various forms with the object of providing the operator with a work area of the correct shape and size to support the garment while it is being sewn and handled. Four examples of standard forms are shown in Figure 13.26.

Work chairs

Sewing for long periods makes great physical demands on the operator and an ergonomically designed work chair can help reduce fatigue significantly. Apart from comfort and support, the chair should allow the operator to work at different distances from the needle, especially when aligning long parts for sewing. Where the operation requires it, the work chair is mounted on rails and can be freely moved backwards or forwards by the operator pushing or pulling against the front edge of the worktable. In some cases, the machine pedal is attached to the chair and travels with it.

Because of development in some quick response systems, many new work stations are being designed to allow the operator to work standing up or seated. However, the majority of operators still work seated at a machine. Although an ergonomically designed work chair is a relatively expensive item, it provides many physical and psychological benefits.

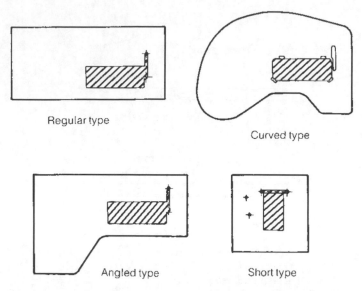

Regular type

Curved type

Angled type

Short type

Fig. 13.26 Sewing machine tables. Regular type: The most widely used machine table for general purposes. Curved type: The size and form allows for the easy manoeuvring of large and heavy components. Angled type: The overhang at the left of the table enables long and unwieldly parts to be positioned and supported during sewing. Short type: This is used when there are restrictions in opening out a garment and/or when only a small area has to be supported while being sewn

Bundle clamps

These, in various forms, hold a bundle of work in the most convenient position for the operator to reach and grasp one component. The clamping position of the bundle is at the end of the components opposite to where the operation(s) are performed. After completing the operation, the part is pushed to the left where it falls between the clamp and the side of the machine. The clamp is mounted on wheels and can be pushed from operator to operator without disturbing the bundle. Figure 13.27 shows an example of a trouser leg clamp which permits the operator to work on the waist area of the leg panel without having to handle the entire leg.

Stackers

A certain percentage of the standard time allowed for an operation is for the disposal and bundling of work after sewing. The time for these elements can be substantially reduced by the use of stackers which automatically remove work from the machine and stack the components in bundles. The two basic types of stackers in general use are:

(1) *Large parts stacker* (Fig. 13.28) These can be mounted at the back or side of the machine and are used for the disposal and stacking of long components such as jacket fronts, skirt panels, trouser legs, etc.

(2) *Small parts stacker*   This type of stacker is used for small parts like collars, cuffs, tabs, etc. and can be mounted at the side or back of the machine. The removal and stacking of work is performed through an extendable arm which slides the sewn component sideways to the stacking rack, where it falls down. The base of the rack automatically adjusts its height so that components have the minimum distance to fall, thus preventing the possibility of them falling in the wrong position.

The actions of the large and small parts stackers can be actuated by the operator or synchronised with the end of the final element in the operation.

Fig. 13.27   Trousers bundle clamp

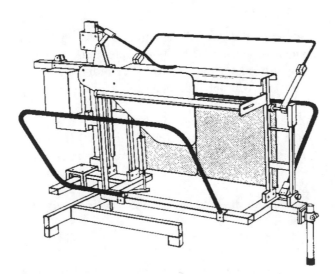

Fig. 13.28   Rear-mounted large parts stacker

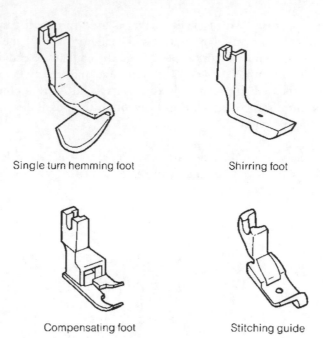

Single turn hemming foot   Shirring foot

Compensating foot   Stitching guide

Fig. 13.29   Special purpose feet. Single turn hemming foot: This folds an edge at the required width and stitches it down at a predetermined distance from the fold. Shirring foot: This gauges in one ply of cloth while it is being joined to another ply. The foot is also called a gauging foot. Compensating foot: The left, right or both fingers of the foot are able to rise or lower according to variations in the thickness being sewn. Stitching guide: This is an example of an edge stitching guide which is built into the foot

Machine attachments

The main class of work aids are those fitted to sewing machines in order to reduce the amount of time for which the operator has to handle or manipulate the work before or during sewing. Apart from reducing handling time, a correctly designed work aid will help the operator maintain consistent standards of quality.

There is a vast selection of work aids available which are purpose-built for specific operations on a wide range of machines. Figures 13.29 to 13.34 show some representative types of attachments and are arranged according to the following categories:

(1) *Feet*   These combine the basic funtion of the foot with the capability of a special operation.
(2) *Folders and binders*   Used for folding and/or joining while simultaneously sewing.
(3) *Stitching and edge guides*   These enable the operator to sew or top-stitch parts at a consistently accurate width.

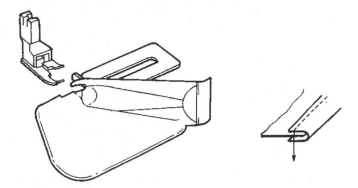

Fig. 13.30 Single turn tape binder. Used in conjunction with a compensating foot, this folder is used for tapes which have a finished edge

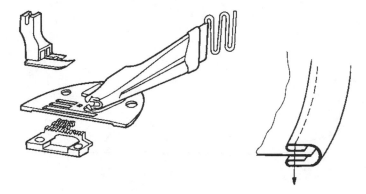

Fig. 13.31 Right-angle double fold binder. The folder is mounted on the throat plate, at right angles to the sewing line. A special feed dog set and foot are parts of the unit which folds in both edges of the tape as it is being bound and sewn

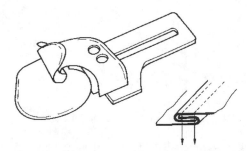

Fig. 13.32 Lap seam folder. Used on two- or three-needle machines, this attachment folds the edges of the two parts being joined and interleaves them while they are sewn

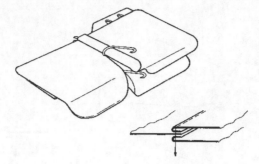

Fig. 13.33 Yoke setter. Used mainly for shirts, this folder turns in the edges of the two yokes and sandwiches the body section between them

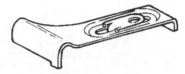

Flat stitching guide

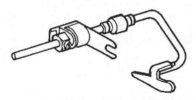

Swing arm stitching guide

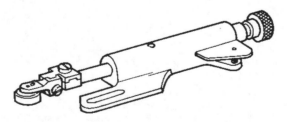

Cylindrical stitching guide

Fig. 13.34 Stitching guides. Flat stitching guide: This is mounted on the bed plate of the machine and the raised left end acts as the edge guide. Swing arm stitching guide: This is mounted on the pressure foot bar and is available with guide arms to the left or right of the needle. The arm, with the guide edge, can be raised or lowered as required. Cylindrical switching guide: The edge guide is a small wheel which enables very sharp contours to be accurately stitched. A spring-locking action engages or releases the guide very quickly

Sewing technology is a broad-based subject dealing with the optimum combination of many different and sometimes critical factors. The most excellent cutting, fusing and pressing is worthless if the garment is not assembled and stitched correctly. Apart from the quality aspects of sewing, productivity must also be considered because efficiency is to a large extent determined by the tools used.

Welding and bonding technology

Welding and bonding technologies have always had a place in the construction of garments but until recently this has been for very specific, and usually specialised, products. With the development of these technologies, however, it is becoming increasingly common to see them applied to general garment types in whole or in part. At one extreme there are examples of outdoor clothing which have in excess of 95% of the seams welded or bonded rather than sewn, and at the other extreme a garment may simply have a logo bonded to the main fabric.

The advantages of such seam creation techniques include increased extensibility and flexibility along with water repellence (no needle holes or thread to act as a wick), but it is arguable that the main advantage comes from reduced seam bulk. Welding or bonding have the advantage of being able to produce very efficient butted or narrowly overlapped seams (Fig. 13.35), thus reducing the thickness of the seam. At the same time, the weight is reduced (by up to 15% at times), the bending rigidity is reduced and the physical irritation caused by the seam is minimised.

Welding

The most common technique for welding textile materials is ultrasonic welding. As with all welding techniques, the material must be caused to melt and flow

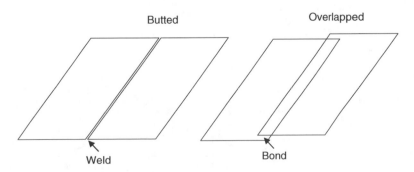

Butted   Overlapped

Weld   Bond

Fig. 13.35 Welded or bonded seam types

together at the joint area. However, welding textile materials differs from welding metal in that no additional material is introduced. The ultrasonic welding machine relies upon acoustic energy to cause vibration within the fabric via the acoustic horn which in turn generates heat due to friction. The oscillating frequency of the horn is typically in the range of 20–30 kHz. These machines are designed for continuous rather than static welding to produce seams.

Bonding

Textile materials are bonded through the application of extruded single-layer thermoplastic adhesive coatings or multi-layered adhesive films. When sandwiched between the fabric plies and pressurised together under moderate heat a serviceable seam is produced, giving the advantages outlined in the introductory section.

Considerations

When utilising welded or bonded seams, it is important to recognise that the peel-strength of these types of seam is lower than that of a sewn seam. In order to overcome this slight drawback it is important to encapsulate the seam ends within the other seams of the garment. This happens more commonly than one might at first imagine: very few free seam ends exist in a garment.

To sum up

Welding and bonding are technologies gaining in application. They offer seams of reduced bulk and weight and are an exciting development in the area of manufacturing technology.

14 Pressing Technology

Introduction

The need to press garments during and at the end of their production is a basic requirement in order to shape and finish them. The processes involved can be divided into two groups:

(1) *Under pressing*   This is the term used to describe the pressing operations performed on garments while they are being made up.
(2) *Top pressing*   This refers to the finishing operations which a garment undergoes after being completely assembled.

Both groups involve a large number of individual processes, their extent determined by the cloth, quality and design of the garment. Irrespective of the number and types of operations involved, the basic components of pressing are the same.

Steam

Steam and heat are necessary to relax the fabric and make it pliable enough to be moulded by manipulation. The combined effect of steam and heat is to slightly soften the fibre structure so that it can take on an alternative shape.

Pressure

When the cloth has been relaxed by steam, pressure is applied which sets the fibres into their new position. An example of the combination of steam and pressure is the pressing of a crease in a pair of trousers.

Drying

After the application of steam and pressure, the component or garment must be

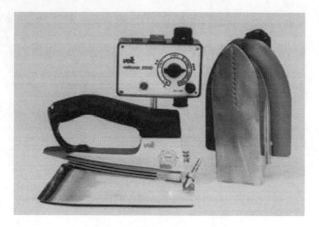

Fig. 14.1   Hand irons

dried and cooled so that the cloth can revert to its normal moisture content and stable condition. This is achieved by a vacuum action which removes the surplus water in the fabric and cools it at the same time. For some pressing operations, hot air or infrared heating is used instead of vacuum for drying.

Time

The length of time the article is subjected to steam, pressure and drying depends on the fabric and the part being pressed; there is an optimum time for each component.

Machinery and equipment

Since the invention of the first mechanically operated pressing machine in 1905, there has been a never-ending development of pressing equipment. Today one prominent manufacturer of this equipment lists over 500 different types of general and special purpose machines ranging from those for one simple operation to combination machines capable of performing every operation required for pressing a man's jacket.

For hundreds of years hand irons were heated on charcoal braziers or coal stoves, with some irons having live charcoal in the body of the iron itself. Although these methods were gradually replaced by gas heating, steam was still generated by lightly wetting the area to be pressed or by pressing through a dampened piece of linen.

The industrial hand irons in current use (Fig. 14.1) are a far cry from the 9 kg (20 lb) monsters wielded by generations of pressers. The two basic types of irons used today are:

(1)   *Dry-iron*   These are lightweight irons weighing about 1.4 kg (3 lb) with a heat range of between 70 and 240 °C and electronic temperature controls that

have a reliable accuracy of ±3 °C. This type of iron is made in a variety of shapes and is mainly used for smoothing or finishing operations where steam is unnecessary. If, for some reason, dampening is required, distilled water can be finely sprayed on to the area with a spray pistol operated by compressed air.

(2) *Electric steam irons*   These are the most commonly used type of hand irons and carry out a wide variety of operations, especially those concerned with under pressing. The iron has a heating element, and steam is fed from a central or independent boiler into the steam chamber in the base of the iron. The steam is superheated by the element and released as required through perforations drilled in the iron soleplate. A micro-switch in a convenient position at the side of, or within, the handle releases the steam.

Under pressing

Basically this type of equipment is either general or special purpose.

General

This can be a unit consisting of a rectangular table with a built-in pressing area or it can be shaped like a domestic ironing board. It is equipped with an iron and connected to a central or independent steam and vacuum supply. Some of these units are also fitted with a shaped form mounted on a swivel arm at the back of the table, which can be pulled into position when required. The operator usually works in a standing position, and the vacuum, and sometimes the release of steam, is controlled by foot pedals. Figure 14.2 shows an example of a general purpose unit.

Special purpose

Apart from hand iron operations, there are many under pressing operations performed on a machine; for example, edge-pressing before top-stitching or simultaneously pressing the shoulders and fusing the shoulder pads into position.

Figure 14.3 shows a 180° carousel machine purpose-built for pressing open the curved seams of a two-piece tailored sleeve. The operator opens the seams with a hand iron and then the lower buck is rotated to the rear of the machine where the seams are finished pressed by the closure of the top buck.

Top pressing

There is an enormous range of pressing machines and equipment for top pressing and finishing, capable either of one operation only or of performing all the operations required to completely top press a garment. There are three different types of action in a pressing machine: scissors, cassette or drawer, and carousel.

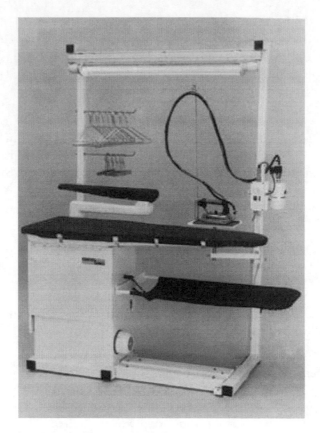

Fig. 14.2　General purpose under pressing unit

Scissors press (Fig. 14.4)

This type of machine has a static lower buck and a conforming top buck which, through a scissor-type leverage action, can be lowered and raised. Each buck has a steam supply and the bottom buck, or sometimes both bucks, are connected to the vacuum supply. Originally these types of machines were manually operated through a system of foot pedals and levers, but today most machines are operated by compressed air which eliminates a great deal of the physical effort previously required. The illustration shows a scissor-type utility press which is a maid of all work in many factories.

Cassette or drawer

These machines are mostly operated in pairs and the principle is that while one machine is pressing, the second is being unloaded and then loaded with unpressed garments. The machine takes its name from the action of the lower buck which moves in a horizontal plane from the operator's front loading position to the back of the machine where the vertically moving top buck is located.

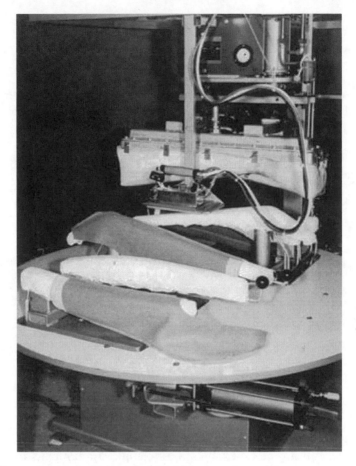

Fig. 14.3 Carousel type under pressing machine

A typical arrangement for this type of machine would be for pressing the backs and fronts of jackets, with the following configuration:

Machine No. 1   Left and right half of back.
Machine No. 2   Left and right front.

At any one time there are four garments on the two machines and the operator would remove a finished jacket after every fourth pressing cycle.

Carousel machines (Fig. 14.5)

Pressing machines with carousel actions are built in three types of buck configurations, the main difference between them being output. As a rule, small carousel presses with one top buck and two bottom bucks have a higher production rate than, say, a machine with two top bucks and four bottom bucks. Regardless of the buck configuration, all carousel presses work on the principle that while one

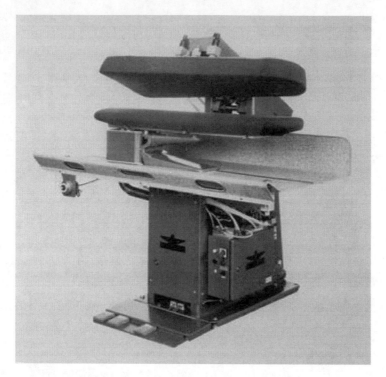

Fig. 14.4 Scissor-type utility press

part is being pressed the operator is preparing the next part. These simultaneous operations are a great time-saver and almost completely eliminate the waiting time involved when pressing on scissor-type machines.

The action of these machines consists of vertically moving top bucks with bottom bucks mounted on a lower plate which rotates through 180° or 120°. The swivelling action of the plate brings the loaded bottom bucks into alignment with the top bucks, while returning another one or two bottom bucks from the pressing site to the operator's position. This rotating action is what gives these machines their name.

The machine illustrated is a 120° carousel used for pressing the left and right fronts of jackets.

There are also pressing units which finish garments in one operation, mostly used for unconstructed garments, i.e. unlined and with little or no fusibles. Two examples of these units are the steam dolly and tunnel-finishing.

Steam dolly (Fig. 14.6)

This is basically a mechanised tailor's dummy consisting of a shaped inflatable nylon bag into which steam and air are blown. The garment is put on to the form and steam is forced through it. Pressurised hot air inflates the nylon body, which

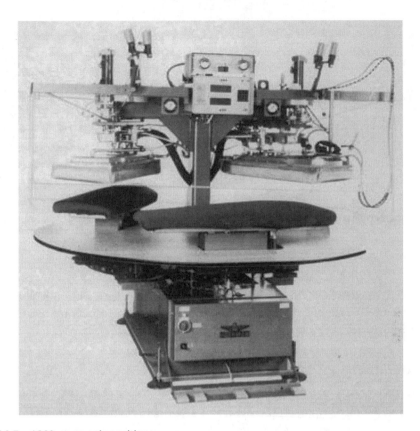

Fig. 14.5 120° carousel machine

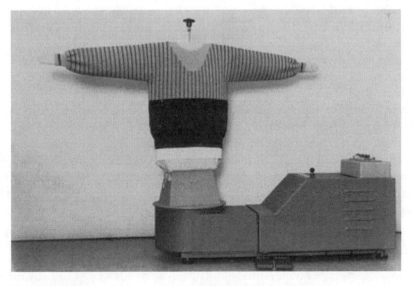

Fig. 14.6 Steam dolly

Fig. 14.7 Tunnel finisher for sweaters

sets and dries the garment. Certain types of garment can be completely finished on the steam dolly while others might require some minor touching-up operations by hand iron.

Tunnel-finishing (Fig. 14.7)

This consists of a conveyer-fed unit through which the garments pass while being steamed and dried. A smaller version is known as a cabinet tunnel which automatically processes separate batches of four or five garments at a time. The production capacity of a cabinet machine is about 10% that of a tunnel unit, and they are mostly used by small factories.

Some other important technological features of modern pressing machinery and equipment include the following.

Controls

Accurate control of the pressing elements is highly important in maintaining a uniform level of quality. On modern machines this is achieved by a microprocessor control which can be programmed for the time, type and sequence of all the elements within a specific pressing operation.

Among other features, these microprocessors control steam and air volumes, vacuum, temperatures and buck pressure on the part being pressed. This flexibility enables the factory to prepare precise programmes for every type of cloth to be pressed.

Handling systems

This subject is now receiving as much attention as handling systems for the sewing room and the same principles apply. Simple robotic arm systems can be attached to the pressing machine to feed the operator with garments in the most convenient way for positioning on the press. After pressing, another arm removes the garment to a holding station for the next operation, or places it into a conveyor where it is transported to its next destination in the pressing line. It is estimated that the reduction in time for garment pick-up and disposal increases productivity by between 15 and 20%.

The boiler room

The boiler room and its distribution systems represent a very substantial investment because of the heavy equipment required to generate and supply the pressing sections with their energy sources. Apart from steam boilers, pressing also needs vacuum turbines, air-compressors, water filtration equipment, and fuel-oil storage and feed systems.

   The outputs of the boiler room have to be distributed throughout the factory and this necessitates a network of pipes for steam, vacuum, compressed air and condensate. Taking everything into account, pressing is probably the highest per capita investment in a clothing factory.

To sum up

Fusing and pressing are the two processes which have the greatest influence on the finished look of a garment. Fusing creates the foundation, and pressing puts the final seal of quality on the garment.

15 Production Technology

Most of the production systems employed in clothing factories are derived from the manual or mechanical systems described in this chapter. Each production system has its own specific operational characteristics in terms of:

* supervision;
* labour;
* quality control;
* productivity;
* throughput time;
* layout.

These factors are examined in the following.

Manual systems

Making through

This is essentially the traditional method of production whereby the entire garment is assembled by one operator. In men's bespoke wear, it is not uncommon for a tailor to perform nearly every operation required to make the garment, including machining, hand work, and pressing.

With this production system the operator would be given a bundle of cut work and would proceed to sew it according to his or her own method of work. Of necessity, the labour required by this system must be highly skilled and versatile, a combination which is becoming exceedingly rare and increasingly expensive. The characteristics of the making through system are:

* *Supervision* The requirements are minimal because the operators decide on their own working methods. At the most a supervisor would provide bundles of work together with some explanation, and then remove the finished work when ready.

- *Labour*   As highly skilled labour is used for the simplest of operations, costs are relatively high when compared with other systems.
- *Quality control*   Obviously this is necessary, but not at the same level as required for garments produced by semi-skilled or unskilled labour.
- *Productivity*   Because of the lack of specialisation, this system is not conducive to high levels of productivity.
- *Throughput time*   This is reduced to a minimum because there is no real necessity for reserves of work other than that actually being sewn by the operator.
- *Layout*   A convenient arrangement of machinery, table space and pressing equipment is all that is required.

This type of system is effective when a very large variety of garments have to be produced in extremely small quantities. A typical application would be in the sewing room of a boutique which produces its own merchandise.

Section or process system

This is a development of the making through system, with the difference that the operators specialise in one major component and sew it from beginning to end. For example, an operator specialising in fronts would assemble the front, set the pockets and perform all the other operations required to finish that particular component.

The sewing room would have a number of sections, each containing versatile operators capable of performing all the operations required for a specific component. The sections are built according to the average garment produced, and include:

- pre-assembling (the preparation of small parts);
- front making;
- back making;
- main assembly (closing, setting collars and sleeves, etc.);
- lining making;
- setting linings;
- finishing operations (buttonholes, blind-stitching, etc.).

Some features of this system are:

- *Supervision*   This is more involved in production and has to ensure the correct movement of work from section to section.
- *Labour*   As labour with varying levels of skill can be used, the system is somewhat cheaper than making through.
- *Quality*   Because of the various levels of operator skill, in-process quality control has to be very thorough.
- *Productivity*   Somewhat higher than the making through system, but still requires skilled operators to perform simple operations within the context of their specialisation.

- *Throughput time* This is longer because of the larger quantities of work in process.
- *Layout* This would be planned according to the process flow of the average garment produced by the factory. All 'one-time' special operations would be performed off-section on machinery that is not a permanent part of a section.

All in all, this is a very efficient system for producing a variety of styles in reasonable quantities. Figure 15.1 shows a typical layout and work flow for this type of system.

Progressive bundle system

This system is exactly what its name implies: a system whereby the garments are gradually assembled as they move through successive sub-assembly and main assembly operations in bundle form. The principles of this system are:

- The various sections are positioned according to the main operation sequence, with each section having a layout according to the sequence of operations required to produce a particular component. For example, the sleeve section could contain the following sequence of operations:

  (1) sew seam;
  (2) press seam;
  (3) blind-stitch hem.

  The amount of machinery for each operation would be determined by the output required.

- A work store is positioned at the start and end of every section and these buffers are used to store work received from a preceding operation, and to hold work completed by that section.
- These work stores or buffers mean that each section is not directly dependent on the preceding section but can absorb slight variations in output because of the stocks held within the section.

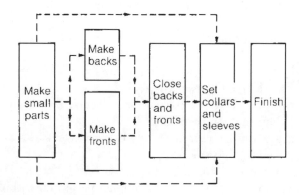

Fig. 15.1 Section system layout

The major features of this system are:

- *Supervision*   This is not just involved in ensuring the correct movement of work between sections, but is concerned with the movement and balance of work within the section.
- *Labour*   This can be of various skill and cost levels because the more complex operations are broken down into a series of small and relatively simple operations.
- *Quality*   In-process quality control is now involved in inspecting individual operations rather than completed components.
- *Productivity*   Because of the breakdown of operations and the possibility of introducing speciality machines, productivity is relatively high compared to that of most other systems.
- *Throughput time*   This is considerably increased because of the amount of work stored at the beginning and end of each section.
- *Layout*   This is particularly important because the end of one section must be positioned adjacent to the start of the section which performs the next series of operations.

The progressive bundle system, while being somewhat cumbersome in operation and requiring large quantities of work in progress, is probably one of the most stable systems as regards output. Unless there is serious absenteeism or prolonged special machine breakdowns, most of the usual hold-ups can be absorbed because of the amounts of work in progress. Balancing and the changeover to new styles is also somewhat simplified, because of the amounts of work held in reserve. When properly managed, the progressive bundle system is versatile and efficient. Figure 15.2 shows a typical layout and work-flow for this system.

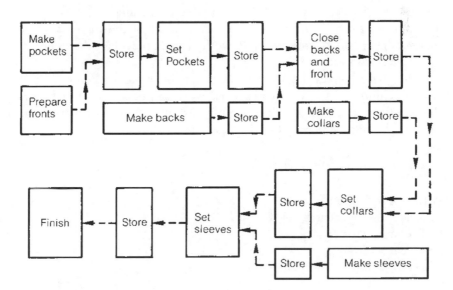

Fig. 15.2   Progressive bundle system layout

Straight line or 'synchro' system

As its name suggests, this system is based on a synchronised flow of work through each stage of producing a garment. Time-synchronisation is the most important factor of this system because the flow of work cannot be synchronised if there are considerable variations in the standard times allowed for all the operations performed on the line. For example, if one operation has a value of 1.5 minutes, then all the other operations in the line must have the same, or a very close, value. The manipulation required to balance the standard times for each operator can sometimes lead to illogical combinations of whole or part operations which are not always conducive to the overall efficiency of individual operators.

The synchro system by its very nature is rigid and particularly vulnerable to absenteeism and machine breakdowns. At all times reserve operators and machines must be available to fill the gaps. In addition, this system requires a sufficient volume of the same type of garment to keep the line in continuous operation.

The basic features of this system are:

- *Supervision* Because of its rigidity, supervisors are very much concerned with keeping the line in balance at all times. Every minor delay could have serious repercussions.
- *Labour* The operators require relatively high skill levels because of the combination of different operations which sometimes have to be performed in order to maintain a time balance between the operations in the line.
- *Quality* In-process quality control must be more alert and intensive because hold-ups caused through quality problems can stop the line in a matter of minutes.
- *Productivity* All things being equal, productivity levels can be very high because of the regular pace of the successive operations.
- *Throughput time* This is very short as a result of the quantity of work in process. There are no intermediate work stores other than the bundles awaiting the next operation.
- *Layout* The simplest layout is the straight line system when one operator is seated behind or opposite the next one. Work can be fed from one operator to the other by gravity chutes or by simply pushing a bundle of work in the right direction along the bench (Fig. 15.3).

To be effective, this system requires:

- volume production;
- accurate line balancing;
- skilled supervision;
- reserve operators;
- reserve machinery and equipment.

If these conditions are fulfilled, the synchro system can be very efficient.

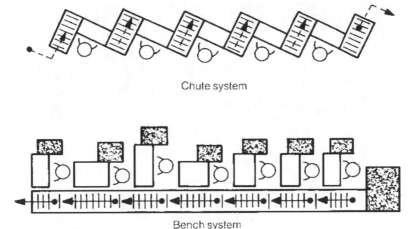

Chute system

Bench system

Fig. 15.3   The synchro system

Mechanical transport systems

Mechanical conveyors have been used in the clothing industry since the early 1920s for transporting work over a fixed route at a set speed. Since their inception they have become an important part of production technology as a result of the application of computerised feed and control systems. The types of system in current use are as follows.

Selective conveyor belt system

The basic features of this system are that it reduces the handling of work to a minimum and maintains the work in process at very low levels. The economic advantages in automatically feeding work containers to an operator and eliminating time-consuming fetch-and-carry methods are self-evident.

A typical conveyor belt system (Fig. 15.4) consists of a main conveyor, a small take-off conveyor and some 30 to 50 work stations positioned either side of the main conveyor. The top belt of the conveyor feeds the work stations, while the lower half returns the completed work which is then fed on to the take-off conveyor and directed to the central work store. This store is open-sided and work can be placed into it from either side. For example, work in process will be stored from the front of the store, while finished work or new work can be handled from the back of the store rack.

The basic operation of this system is:

Each operator is provided with two boxes of work; when the processing of one box has been completed the operator places it on the lower band of the conveyor and moves the reserve box to the working position. This causes the work station light to be illuminated on the control panel, indicating to the loading operator controlling the feed and storage of work that additional work is required at that

Fig. 15.4   Conveyor belt system

station. The loading operator then places a box of work on the top band of the conveyor and presses the push button under the station indicator light. The work is delivered to the operator who is notified by a flashing light that another box is on the way. When the box reaches the work station the operator places it on the reserve box position. The red light then goes out on the control panel and the control operator knows that as long as this light is out, the operator has work in reserve.

A more recent development is where the storage and dispatch of work is controlled by a computer. The tote boxes are positioned and moved automatically by a robotic type of stacker and retriever, working according to instructions supplied by the computer.

- *Supervision*   The supervisor is relieved of the task of work feeding and is able to spend more time working with the operators.
- *Labour*   All grades and rates.
- *Quality control*   In-process systems are operated.
- *Productivity*   Reasonably high because in an efficiently run unit there is a continual flow of work.
- *Throughput time*   Still measured in days because of the amount of work in process.
- *Layout*   A very compact straight line.

The selective conveyor belt system requires a great deal of planning and control if it is to give good results. However, if these functions are performed effectively, the system provides a highly efficient and economic method for the simultaneous production of different styles in varying quantities.

Unit production system (UPS)

As a mechanical system this has been in use for many years, but a major advance was made in 1983 when computers were first used to plan, control and direct the flow of work through the system.

The essential features of this type of system are:

(1)   The unit of production is a single garment and not bundles.
(2)   The garment components are automatically transported from work station to work station according to a predetermined sequence.
(3)   The work stations are so constructed that the components are presented as close as possible to the operator's left hand in order to reduce the amount of movement required to grasp and position the component to be sewn.

The operational principles are as follows:

All the components for one garment are loaded into a carrier at a work station specially designed for this purpose. The carrier itself is divided into sections, with each section having a quick-release retaining clamp which prevents the components from falling out during movement through the system. When a batch of garments has been loaded into carriers they are fed past a mechanical or electronic device which records the number of the carrier and addresses it to its first destination. Some of the more intelligent systems address the carriers with all the destinations they will have to pass through to completion.

The loaded carriers are then fed on to the main powered line which continually circulates between the rows of machines. This main, or head, line is connected to each work station by junctions which open automatically if the work on a carrier is addressed to that particular station. The carrier is directed to the left side of the operator and waits its turn along with the other carriers in the station (Fig. 15.5).

When the operator has completed work on one carrier, a push button at the side of the sewing machine is pressed and this actuates a mechanism which transports the carrier back to the main line. As one carrier leaves the station, another is automatically fed in to take its place. When the carrier leaves the station it is recorded on the data collection system, and then addressed to its next destination.

The marked advantages of this type of system are:

•   Bundle handling on the part of the operator is completely eliminated.
•   The time involved in the pick-up of work and its disposal is reduced to the minimum possible.
•   Output is automatically recorded, thus eliminating the necessity for the operator to register work.

- The computerised systems automatically balance the work between stations performing the same operation.
- Up to 40 styles can be produced simultaneously on one system.
- *Supervision* The supervisor is freed to work with the operators.
- *Labour* All grades and all rates.
- *Quality control* In-process inspection stations are built into the line and the inspector is able to return faulty work via the system to the operator concerned.
- *Throughput time* This is measured in hours instead of days because of the low amounts of work in hand.
- *Productivity* High because the operators are working in a 'paced' environment which enables them to develop faster working rhythms.
- *Layout* Can be of any form suitable to the available area.

Unit production systems require substantial investments which are not always justified by conventional pay-back calculations. Apart from the measurable tangible

Fig. 15.5 UPS work station

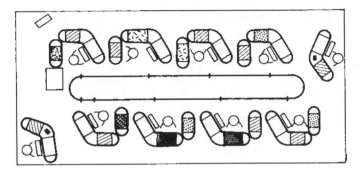

Fig. 15.6 Quick response system layout

benefits, UPSs also have many intangible benefits such as a more orderly and controlled flow of work, and the ability via the control computer of simulating the production situation some time in advance. These intangibles are difficult to measure, but in themselves make a very positive contribution to the overall viability of the unit.

All things considered, unit production systems have major advantages over all the other manual and mechanical systems used for the mass production of clothing. Most importantly, they provide a clothing factory with the capability to respond quickly to any changes which might occur. In the fast-moving fashion business, this is essential.

Quick response system (Fig. 15.6)

This system was first developed in Japan to enable quick responses to be made to market changes, especially when orders for individual styles were in small lots. Each work station is equipped with two to four machines and the operator will take the garment through the required operations, including pressing, before it is transported to the next work station.

Some of the basic machinery is duplicated in different stations, and if there is a bottleneck in one section the overload is automatically transported to other stations where operator capacity is available.

All the parts for one garment are loaded into a hanging clamp attached to the trolley and, in theory, there should only be one garment at each work station. Work is transported by a computer-controlled, overhead trolley system and each station has an individual controller which provides the operator with information on the style being worked on. This information comes from an information card which accompanies each trolley.

A less sophisticated version of QRS uses a wheeled trolley which contains the components for one garment and is pushed along the floor from operator to operator.

Another feature of QRS is that all the operators work in a standing position so that they can move quickly from one machine to another within their own work station. Machine heights are adjusted accordingly and touch-pads and knee-high controls are used instead of conventional foot pedals.

- *Supervision*   The supervisor is freed to work with the operators.
- *Labour*   Of necessity the operators must be highly skilled in the operation of all the different machines in one work station.
- *Quality*   In-process inspection stations are built into the line and the inspector is able to return faulty work via the system to the operator concerned.
- *Productivity*   This is very high because the operator handles the garment once only for a number of operations, instead of once for each operation.
- *Throughput time*   As there are so few garments on the line throughput time is extremely short, which is the objective of this system.
- *Layout*   A typical unit would have eight work stations arranged around the transport system.

There is no doubt that this type of system is one of the best answers to the garment production revolution which is becoming more apparent every day. Fashion changes are becoming more frequent and as a consequence order lots are proportionately smaller. A production system which enables changeovers to be made in the minimum of time is ideally suited to this new and dynamic situation.

To sum up

There are materials movement systems to suit every conceivable type of requirement, and the objective of them all is to reduce the non-productive time involved in work transport and handling at the work station.

16 Warehousing

The final group of operations in the production of clothing prepares finished merchandise for delivery to the customer. These operations come under the heading of materials handling systems and are no less important than other systems used in the factory. The warehouse is an integral link in the manufacturing chain and should receive the same thought and planning as is given to other production systems.

The main sequence of operations in a finished goods warehouse is:

- receiving finished goods from the factory;
- checking quantities and sorting into styles, colours and sizes;
- storing the garments in pre-planned locations;
- allocating the garments according to customers' orders;
- packing or preparing the garments for delivery to customers;
- organising deliveries.

The operational elements of large-scale warehousing are the warehouse itself and the handling, storage and packing equipment.

The warehouse

The planning and layout of the warehouse would take into account:

- the types of garments to be warehoused and whether they are stored in hanging or boxed form, or a combination of both;
- the highest stock levels to be held in the warehouse;
- the amount of in and out garment traffic at peak times;
- the sorting and allocation facilities required if small orders of many different styles have to be prepared and combined for individual customers;
- working areas and equipment for bagging, ticketing and bulk packing;
- the logical placement of adequate space for the receipt and dispatch of merchandise;
- the layout of the stores to provide a direct flow of garments from receipt to dispatch.

Handling equipment

Materials handling systems for clothing factories are classified under three headings:

(1) *Manual or free systems*   These systems, as the name suggests, are based on the movement of merchandise by physical effort. A simple example of a manual system for hanging goods is a trolley holding the garments being pushed along an overhead suspended rail.

(2) *Powered systems*   These can be railed systems with trolleys for hanging goods or powered conveyor tables for boxed goods. Some of the more sophisticated powered systems are computer controlled and automatically direct trolleys in and out of the storage and working areas of the warehouse (Fig. 16.1).

(3) *Power and free systems*   These are systems where part is powered and the rest is operated manually. A typical system would power the trolleys adjacent to the storage areas, from where they would be manually pushed into the storage area or unloaded on to rails or racked shelving.

Fig. 16.1   Computer-controlled routing system

Fig. 16.2 Transport and storage system – flat-packed garments

Storage equipment

Boxed goods

These are generally stored in racked shelving systems or in cartons (Fig. 16.2). Because of the compactness of the packed unit and the protection afforded by the outer covering, the storage density is high compared to that of hanging goods. The rail system used for moving the goods can be manually or power operated.

Hanging goods

There are basically two types of rail storage systems for hanging goods and the system employed depends on order size and the variety of merchandise within each order, i.e. whether the order consists of a large quantity of one style or small quantities of many styles.

Static system

This consists of fixed rails, with the storage and retrieval of hanging goods performed physically. In order to pick-off or select garments, the picker walks along the lengths of rail, locates the required garments and then manually loads them on to a moveable rail or suspended trolley. A static rail storage system in conjunction with a powered, or power and free, transport system is used where large orders for the same garment have to be shipped in bulk to the customer.

Dynamic system

The factory warehouse often has to break down a number of large orders for different styles into small amounts for distribution to, say, a chain of retail shops. For this type of goods handling, the location and retrieval system has to be very speedy in order to pick-off a variety of small orders efficiently.

A widely used system is a computer-controlled carousel which operates as follows. The carousel is loaded with garments which have been pre-sorted for style, colour and size. Each batch is loaded on to a section of the carousel and the details and position of the garments are recorded on the computer. When the operator enters a request for specific garments, the carousel starts revolving until the section containing those garments arrives in the unloading area. The operator then unloads the garments and directs them, via another powered rail system, to their next destination.

Packing equipment

Bagging

Most garments are packed in plastic bags, either at the end of production or when they enter the finished goods stores. Products like shirts and underwear are usually bagged and boxed directly after final inspection and enter the stores in pre-packed form. For these and similar types of product there are many automatic machines available.

Other hanging garments such as jackets, dresses and skirts are usually bagged when they enter the stores and there is a variety of equipment for this purpose.

Manual machines

The garment is hung within the machine and the flat plastic tube, which comes from a roll mounted over the machine, is pulled down over the garment. The top of the tube is cut and heat sealed and the garment withdrawn from the machine.

Semi-automatic machines

These operate on the same principle as the manual machine, but the plastic tube is automatically pulled down over the garment. The operator still has to load and unload the machine and activate the cutting and sealing mechanism.

Fully automatic machines

The hanging garments are loaded on to a powered spiral drive which feeds the garments one at a time into the bagging machine. After bagging and sealing, the garments are automatically positioned on to another spiral drive which transports them to waiting trolleys or storage rails. The operation is entirely automatic and some of the more modern machines can bag and seal some 500 garments per hour.

Boxing

When boxed or hanging garments have to be transported in bulk packed form, the most commonly used medium is a carton made of strong corrugated material. The garments or boxes are packed into the carton which can either be sealed by contact adhesive paper tape or bound with a plastic tape. There are manual and automatic machines available for both.

Transportation issues

The global distribution of clothing manufacturers and the distance from the eventual market for which the garments are produced has placed increasing importance on the choice of transportation method, and this affects the choice of packaging. If we consider the problem from a time perspective, it is important to minimise the time spent in transit by the garments; from a volume perspective, it is important to maximise the volume of goods transported in one voyage. One may therefore be lead to think that we should cram as many garments as possible on to an airplane – highest volume, shortest time. But this is a high-cost approach which has to be evaluated carefully. So we see most commonly a combination of land and sea transportation.

To maximise the volume of garments in transit, vacuum packing of high numbers of garments is a proven technology. However, the after-transit processing costs (re-pressing, hanging and arranging) have to be considered. Indeed, for some garment types these costs are so high that a more recent approach is the total opposite of this. Air-packing garments (think of a bag of washed salad leaves) ensures that they are not distorted in transit and, although the volume of garments delivered in one voyage is reduced, this is offset by the lower cost of re-processing when they arrive at the point of consumption. At the extreme end of the scale, garments are required to arrive at the retailer with all ticketing correctly attached, hung and prepared for presentation, thus reducing further the lead time of garment from manufacture to retail.

Transportation to where?

As described in the early part of this chapter, the warehouse has traditionally provided a central storage and distribution function. However, with the increasing need to compress the lead time of garment delivery, it is becoming necessary for alternative distribution networks to be used in order to reduce transport and storage time (Fig. 16.3). While nobody wants to hold stock (and if they have to, the volume held is at least minimised), it is possible that the manufacturer will

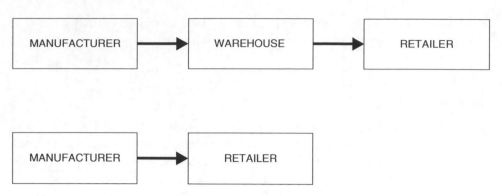

Fig. 16.3   The distribution chain

now hold and then deliver direct to retail stores, thus negating a link in the distribution chain.

Clearly removing this link is an advantage but it brings with it the need for improved communications, especially when a retailer is taking products from several manufacturers.

To sum up

A well-planned and efficiently operated warehouse will provide effective service for the production department and for the company's customers. Alternative distribution networks go straight to store and help reduce garment lead times.

The exploitation of production technology

The payback period

The payback period has long been the traditional method for assessing the financial return on any capital investment. Traditionally the clothing industry has expected an investment to pay for itself within two years. Two years was accepted as a short period, and for manufacturers of staple products reflected a rather short-term view. If a new technology would not pay for itself within two years then it would not be purchased, and thus they missed out on some opportunities. For example, under the following calculation the technology would not be purchased:

Cost of technology = 8000

Annual savings   = 2000/year

Payback period   = cost of technology $= \dfrac{8000}{2000} = 4$ years

Table 16.1   Some less tangible benefits

Benefit	Possible metric
Improved quality	Reduced return to manufacturer (RTM-rework)
	Increased sales through reputation
Increased manufacturing flexibility	Increased market share
	Reduced set-up/changeover time = cost
Improved market standing	
Reduced stock	Lower working capital in raw materials/WIP
	Reduced property expenditure through reduced storage

The double whammy of asymmetric assessment and high hurdle rates

This short payback period can be considered a 'high hurdle rate' inasmuch that for high-value investments the annual savings will have to be great in order to meet the short payback period (even with slight allowances for the size of the project, payback periods of three years are about as high as the industry goes). When combined with another major obstacle to accurate investment appraisal, the evaluation of intangible benefits, we have a serious restriction to the full exploitation of technology by long-run, staple product manufacturers that was acute and still exists today. Asymmetric assessment is a term that describes the imbalance when hard-to-measure/value intangible benefits (Table 16.1) are weighed against the easily quantifiable investment costs. This 'double whammy' of limitations often results in the missing of an opportunity to invest in appropriate production technology.

However, the converse is also true today. At the opposite extreme to staple product manufacturers we have those organisations concerned with fashion products – 'fast fashion' being an acute example of this. These manufacturers have product runs which vary so much (and are so short) that it is even less likely that any investment in technology, when assessed by the payback period method, will make a return on that investment before the product run is finished and the technology faces the possibility of becoming redundant.

It has unfortunately never been uncommon to see stockpiles of redundant machinery on the premises of clothing manufacturers. Without the luxury of time, the decision as to whether or not to acquire a new technology takes on a more entrepreneurial bent. Manufacturers must rely on gut instinct to ensure that they do not miss an opportunity through lack of investment.

Alternative approaches

Without the luxury of investment appraisal, are there alternative approaches to acquiring the required technologies that are less risky or draining of resources?

It is arguable that, with the reduction of the need for specialised machinery development (because of reduced operation specialisation with the shorter product run), less specialised machinery that offers greater flexibility is being increasingly developed and made available to organisations. There is more reliance on operator skill and machine flexibility, and the risk of technology redundancy is lessened. At the same time, the continued development of the operators becomes necessary. The true value of a developed training school is apparent: people are the specialised technology.

Leasing technology rather than buying it outright has always been a possibility but is a more attractive proposition when the expected useful lifetime of that technology is so short. An approach that was once of limited use because of short-term costs now has much more to recommend it.

Large organisations that manufacture several product types (perhaps in distinct production units) must ensure that the bank of technology they have is shared between users. This necessitates a well-maintained database of available technologies and a practical distribution network.

To sum up

A more entrepreneurial approach is needed to the exploitation of technology. The traditional payback method of appraising capital investment is redundant in today's manufacturing climate. Full use has to be made of the operator as a 'flexible technology' and alternative means of acquiring machinery.

Part 4

ENGINEERING AND QUALITY CONTROL

17 Production Engineering

Introduction

Production engineering is concerned with the design, improvement and installation of integrated systems of manpower, materials and equipment. It draws on specialised diagnostic and measurement techniques to develop and specify systems and evaluate their results.

Apart from the design of planning and control systems, the production engineering function in a clothing factory is also responsible for, among others, the following activities:

- setting time standards;
- the design and administration of incentive schemes;
- planning the layouts for production areas, offices, stores, warehouses, etc;
- evaluating the performance of machinery and equipment which is being considered for purchase;
- designing special purpose fixtures and fittings;
- providing consultancy services for all departments in the company.

A technique central to production engineering is work study and it is probably the most effective tool available to management for measuring and diagnosing working situations. While work study is widely accepted at the production level, it can also be profitably applied to other departments in the factory including:

- service departments;
- warehouses and stores;
- general administration;
- planning and control functions of all types.

Some of the main principles and techniques of work study are examined here.

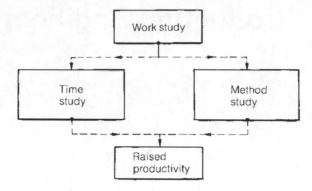

Fig. 17.1 The components of work study

Work study

The fundamental concept of work study is to establish and handle facts in a systematic and disciplined manner. There are two specialised techniques used for these purposes (Fig. 17.1):

(1) *Method study*   An investigative technique used to determine the best way of doing a job.
(2) *Time study (work measurement)*   To establish how long a job should take.

Used together these techniques can influence the following factors:

- the lowering of costs;
- productivity ratios;
- manufacturing profitability;
- the partial or entire elimination of unnecessary work;
- the setting of equitable work loads;
- the determination of performance standards and methods for checking achievements.

Method study

This is the general name given to a problem-solving technique which is used to analyse and solve problems concerned with methods. Some examples of its application are:

(1) designing work stations which enable operators to reach high levels of efficiency;
(2) developing layouts for sections, offices and complete factories;
(3) improving materials flow in stores, warehouses and production areas;
(4) planning the best routes for the movement of people;
(5) developing systems for various functions, right down to the design of the forms to be used.

Method study varies in scale and precision depending on the job or function under examination. For regular sewing operations a very detailed motion study is made of the operator's movements, and these are analysed to establish the most efficient series of motions. Where sewing operations have a short cycle and are repeated thousands of times a day, the operation is recorded by video camera and then analysed through slow motion screenings.

For the analysis of the working methods of, say, a raw materials store, a broader-based technique is used which involves the observation and recording of activities and an analysis of the movement of people and materials. Because of the questioning procedures of method study, unnecessary and wasteful activities are easily discovered and can be eliminated in improved methods.

Time study (work measurement)

All planning and control systems are based on facts and one of the most important of these is the work value of each job. The 'work value' is the product of two factors:

(1) *Value* This is the rate paid to the operator who performs the job, the rate being determined by negotiations, wages agreements, legislation, etc.
(2) *Time* This is the time allowed for the job to be completed at the defined level of quality. The time factor for the job is established through work measurement.

Work value is used for many purposes, including garment costings, budgets and operational profitability, and as a basis for some types of incentive schemes. Time is the central axis of all planning and is used for calculating:

- how many operators are required for each operation in order to perform all the operations necessary for a particular batch of work;
- the number of machines required for each operation;
- the balance between different sections in the factory;
- the allocation of production run durations;
- delivery times to customers;
- labour budgets;
- the parameters of planning and control.

For many years the basic tool used to measure time was the stopwatch, but although it still has some uses, it is gradually being replaced by predetermined motion time systems (PMTS). These systems consist of libraries holding the standard times for all the elements concerned with work. The data can exist in the form of reference tables or can be computerised, and it provides the work study engineer with an accurate and objective method of establishing standard times. Some of the more sophisticated computerised systems also have a graphic capability which enables the work study engineer to simulate alternative motion patterns at the work place in order to develop the most efficient method of working.

Apart from sewing operations, PMTS are also used for pressing operations and some cutting operations.

When the two component parts of work study are operated conjointly, the result is an improvement in working method and in the time allowed for doing the job.

Time standards and incentive schemes

Time standards

The actual time allowed for an operation not only includes the time for the operational elements but also the time for other factors connected with work and the operation itself. Some of the allowances generally given are (Fig. 17.2):

- *Personal allowance*   This is to cover personal needs and an element of rest.
- *Contingency allowance*   The time an operator has to spend consulting the supervisor or talking to a quality control supervisor.
- *Operational and environmental allowances*
  ○ *Thread and bobbin changes*   An allowance is made for the frequency of change and the number of items involved.
  ○ *Other allowances*   Physical effort, visual concentration and posture, and working conditions in and around the station are also taken into account.

For example, an operation having a basic time of 1.00 minute and allowances totalling 20% would have a standard time of 1.20 minutes. (Time standards are calculated on the basis of a centi-minute.) The operator could receive the time standard in various forms:

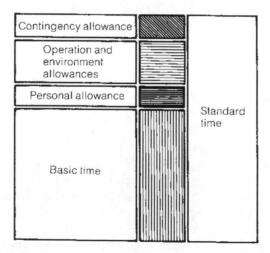

Fig. 17.2   The components of a standard time

- as the number of operations per hour;
- as the number of operations per net working day;
- as a monetary value per operation for all operations performed;
- as a monetary value per operation for all operations performed over a set number in a given time.

Thus, an operator working eight hours net per day and performing an operation with a time standard of 1.20 minutes would be expected to do at least 400 of these operations in a full day.

Whatever system is used to represent standard time, the object is to provide a basis for incentive schemes.

Incentive schemes

Although there are conflicting attitudes regarding payment by results, well-engineered incentive schemes can make a positive contribution to the achievement of high production levels. For management there are two important advantages emanating from sound incentive schemes:

(1) The work load on management and supervision is somewhat reduced, enabling them to concentrate more on organisation and quality than on 'pushing' work.
(2) Management must keep on their toes because any failure of service or work flow will affect the earnings of operators.

So the first principle is that healthy incentive schemes are a result of healthy management.

Principles

Basically an incentive scheme is a method of payment by results, and the principles governing schemes are:

- The smaller the group, the greater the incentive; as a general rule, the best incentive is the individual incentive.
- Reward should be proportional to effort.
- Equal effort should be rewarded by equal payment.
- The knowledge of results should be as close as possible to the time when the efforts were made. Ideally an operator should receive a statement of premium earnings for one day on the following day.
- Normal performance should be rewarded by basic pay only. Incentive payments should ideally start when normal performance has been achieved.
- An incentive scheme should be as simple as possible to understand. The simpler the scheme, the greater the incentive.
- An operator should be able to calculate his or her own earnings.
- The scheme itself should be simple to administer.

- Most importantly, issues regarding incentive schemes should be decided on according to the principles involved and not as a result of bargaining power, internal politics or other influences.
- Incentive schemes will help good managers to manage better, but will not do anything for what is basically poor management.

Premium payments

In most instances premium payments commence when the 'norm' for the operation has been achieved. The basic method of calculation is demonstrated in the following example:

(a) Standard time for the operation: 1.25 mins.
(b) Net working time per day: 480 mins.
(c) The norm is equal to the net working time divided by the standard time or: $480 \div 1.25 = 384$ operations.
(d) The operator would therefore receive a premium payment for every operation over and above 384 during a period of 480 mins.
(e) If, for example, the operator has performed 480 operations during the day, the quantity that stands to earn premium is $480 - 384$ which equals 96 units.
(f) Therefore the premium rate is:

$$\frac{96}{384} = 25\% \text{ (or 125\% performance)}$$

(g) Payments under premium bonus systems are based on a guaranteed hourly or daily rate or base which is sometimes called the fall-back rate. Where for reasons not under the control of the operator premium level performance is not achieved, the operator would receive the base rate only. At premium level performance, the premium payment would be calculated as a percentage of the base rate.

Types of schemes

The conventional types of incentive scheme are:

(1) Payment to the individual operator according to the results achieved. This category is the most widely used for direct production operators.
(2) Payment to individual workers according to the results of a group to which the workers belong. This type of scheme could be applied in a finished garment warehouse where a number of people have to work together in order to prepare merchandise for delivery.
(3) Payment for the results achieved by others to which the worker has made an indirect contribution. For example, if the factory employs a manual work transport system, then those workers responsible for moving work from

section to section or from operator to operator would qualify for this type of premium payment.

Multi-factor schemes

Supervisors are responsible for a number of functions and a premium scheme tries to reward them for all-round achievements rather than just for output. Some of the factors which can be incorporated into such a scheme are:

- output of the section;
- value of the total time produced by the section in relation to the total attendance time of the section;
- relationship between the attendance time of the section and the time actually worked by the section – this refers to time lost by reasons over which the supervisor has direct control;
- overall quality rating of the work produced by the section;
- meeting targets on time;
- cleanliness and tidiness of the section;
- punctuality and absenteeism rate of the operators in the section;
- learner operators in the section.

Each factor is given a weighting according to its relative importance, and the premium is paid accordingly. This type of scheme should ideally have no more than four factors. Table 17.1 shows a typical combination where the planned average premium level for supervisors is 30%.

The premium value is determined by the difference between the planned level and the actual achievement. If, for example, the output of the supervisor's section were 10% more than planned, the premium value for this particular factor would be 1.1×10.5 per cent, or 11.55%. Thus extra output would be rewarded, but the total premium paid to the supervisor would still represent the levels reached in all the factors.

Management bonus schemes

There are many types of monetary and non-monetary incentive schemes for management, and their applications depend on individual circumstances and choice.

Table 17.1 Typical premium levels for a multi-factor scheme

Factor	Rated value %	Premium value
Output	35	10.5
Quality	35	10.5
Productivity	20	6.0
Good housekeeping	10	3.0
Total	100	30.0

Generally these schemes are of the multi-factor type and are directed towards rewarding the overall results achieved by factory and department managers.

Some of the factors which can be incorporated into management incentive schemes are:

- the operational profits of the department or factory;
- the trading profit of the company;
- savings in budgeted costs;
- use of materials.

Economics of incentive schemes

The central principle is that the payment basis must be fair to both employer and employee. In other words, both sides must enjoy the profits which result from output over and above the set standards.

For the operator, the relationship between output and reward is very direct. An operator working on a one-to-one incentive scheme knows that every 1% of output above the norm will pay 1% premium. Thus, an operator with a day rate of 40.00 and a norm of 360 operations, achieving a performance of 125% or 450 operations, will receive as premium 25% of the day rate, i.e. 10.00 for the extra output of 90 units. So as far as the operator is concerned, the indirect piece rate is the day rate of 40.00 divided by the norm of 360 operations, which is equal to 0.11 per unit.

However, the actual cost of the same operation for the employer involves consideration of the following factors:

(1) The norm for the operation is 360 operations per day.
(2) The guaranteed day rate for the operator is 40.00 per day.
(3) The variable overheads for the operator are, say, 25% of the total earnings of the operator. These overheads include National Insurance, holiday pay, etc.
(4) The fixed overheads are, say, 60% of the operator's day rate. These overheads do not vary according to output or earnings and include items such as rent, rates and depreciation.

Therefore the cost of this particular operation for the employer is:

Day rate	40.00
Variable overheads (25% of total salary)	10.00
Fixed overheads (60% of day rate)	24.00
Total	74.00

So if the standard performance is 360 per day, the unit cost is 74.00 ÷ 360 or 0.205.

Assuming that the operator achieves a performance level of 125%, the unit cost would be:

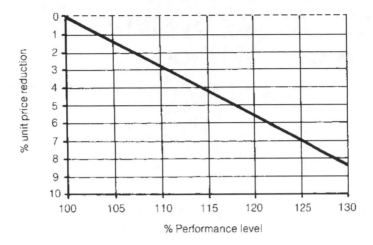

Fig. 17.3   The relationship between cost and performance

Day rate	40.00
25% premium	10.00
Total earnings	50.00
Variable overheads (25% × 50.00)	12.50
Fixed overheads (60% × 40.00)	24.00
Total cost	86.50

If the output at 125% performance is equivalent to 450 operations, the unit cost would be 86.50 ÷ 450 = 0.192 or 0.013 less per unit when compared to the standard cost. In real terms this means that the total unit cost for the employer has been reduced by 6.34% and Figure 17.3 shows how unit costs decrease as the operator's output increases.

There are two conclusions regarding premium payments and unit costs:

(1)   As long as the standard time allowed for the specified method and required quality level is accurate, there should not be any limit on the earnings of operators.
(2)   The more the operator earns, the lower are the unit costs for the employer.

Therefore it is in the interests of both sides that output should be as high as possible.

To sum up

Despite their familiarity and long history of evolution, there is no subject more controversial for employers and employees than incentive schemes. This does not mean that they are of limited value. Like everything else in a clothing factory, their value can only be judged by results.

18 Quality Systems and Methods

Introduction

Quality control is one of the terms used to cover the procedures concerned with the planning and control of quality. Terms such as statistical quality control (SQC) and statistical process control (SPC) are modern tools used to monitor production. Terms such as total quality control (TQC) and TQM (total quality management) are also used. All of them have similar functions. Quality control by any name is basically a systematic regulatory process which:

- establishes standards appropriate to the quality objectives of the company;
- has techniques for measuring the degree of conformity to these standards;
- uses statistical methods for analysing the significance of deviations from these standards;
- reports on the findings of the analyses and, when necessary, recommends and follows up on corrective procedures.

Before examining the individual parts of this in more detail, the total function of quality control has to be located within the context and hierarchy of factory organisation.

Quality

The word 'quality' itself implies a degree of excellence the nature of which is dependent on the reasons for the garment being purchased. A term very often used to describe the quality characteristics of a garment, which together provide the reason for purchasing it, is 'fitness for purpose' and A.J. Chuter (4) has defined this as being:

- quality of design;
- quality of conformance;
- quality of delivery and service.

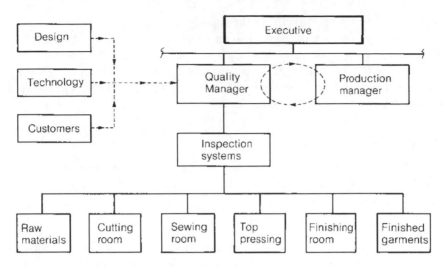

Fig. 18.1   Status of the quality manager

This definition contains what should be the total application of quality control in a clothing factory.

Hierarchy

The ultimate responsibility for the quality of garments produced in a factory lies with top management. Obviously members of the top management team cannot personally co-ordinate all the day to-day activities of quality control, and in conventional organisations they delegate most of this responsibility to a specialist function: the quality manager (Fig. 18.1).

The status of quality managers within organisations must be high enough for their views and opinions to be considered at top management levels, and only a high-ranking executive can arbitrate on the sometimes conflicting interests other managers have with the quality manager. Ideally the total responsibility for garment quality should be vested in one executive only, who is sufficiently distanced from the daily problems of the factory to take an objective view of events.

Ensuring the correct hierarchical status for the quality manager is one of the fundamental rules for the effective operation of quality control systems.

The quality department

Most of the routine decisions will be made by the quality manager who will have, among other qualifications, an in-depth understanding of the company's products and will be highly conversant with customers' attitudes and requirements regarding garment quality.

The inspectors employed by the department work in various sections of the factory, each being responsible for a specific pre-production or production activity. They all report directly to the quality manager and not to the managers or supervisors of various sections or departments, because inspectors do not have direct control over production workers but act in a strictly advisory capacity. Responsibility for the quality of the operations coming off a section belongs to the production supervisor or departmental manager, but they work closely with the inspection team to maintain standards.

Quality audit

The work passed by inspectors is also subject to audit by means of a random sample drawn at specified intervals from the work passed by each inspector. The objectives of this audit are twofold:

(1) to ensure that a minimum of faulty work is being let through;
(2) to verify whether the specified standards are being interpreted correctly by the inspector, meaning neither too rigorously nor too slackly.

Quality monitor

This can be considered as a high-level audit performed at management level, and takes place at regular intervals – say, once a week. Typically the participants are the executive responsible for quality and the production and quality managers, together with the chief technologist. A random sample of the latest production is taken from the finished goods warehouse and collectively appraised, with discussion on the overall quality.

The exchange of views can lead to the highlighting of consistently weak but passable points, or the indications of a possible downward trend. Alternatively, agreement might be reached on the use of a new or different process technology which could improve existing quality without an increase in cost, or a cost reduction exercise that would not affect quality.

Quality monitors provide managers and technologists with a regular and up-to-date feedback regarding the overall effectiveness of their own sphere of operations. An example of an acceptable quality limit (AQL) that demonstrates this is given later in the chapter.

Total quality management

Many organisations are pursuing a quality management strategy in order to secure competitive advantage and deliver superior performance. It is often followed by a declared intention to achieve total quality management (TQM).

Total quality management is not a new concept. It has been around since the mid 1960s but it is only from the mid 1990s that it has started to be implemented in the UK. Within total quality management there are external customers who are the ones that buy the company's products, and internal customers who are the people employed within the organisation where each one is the customer of another. It operates on the principle that if it is faulty then do not buy it. People within the organisation are trained to appreciate this fact. If they are unhappy with

Fig. 18.2   A quality circle

the quality they are receiving from another department or from another machine on an assembly line, they are empowered to stop the operation until the quality problem has been looked at and dealt with by the appropriate authority.

Quality circles

Quality circles (Fig 18.2) are a critical element of TQM and have been fundamental in helping to solve production-related problems. They consist of a team of usually four to ten people, all volunteers, who work together for this one common objective. Together they can be a formidable force in reducing problems that occur within the organisation.

A much wider range of solutions can be generated if there are more people involved. Individual ideas can be built upon as one idea can be an extension of another. A group will bring more information and experience to bear on an unstructured problem, and during the life of the team increased creativity and more risky solutions can be enacted. The formation of such teams enables the manager to concentrate on the strategic planning of the business because the system frees up time that can be allocated for that purpose.

Sometimes members of the group suggest changes to an operation performed in another unit that supplies them with work that would help them improve their own quality performance. The group may also discuss any factors in their working environment which are not conducive to comfort and performance. Quality circles and other similar activities are all directed towards involving operators and supervisors in the acceptance of personal and collective responsibility for quality.

Improving quality at the needle point

The steps to improving garment quality at the needle point start from the realisation that every individual machinist is his or her own manager and is thus responsible for his or her own work. The management team has the responsibility of shaping and developing the environment to enable the machine operative to work as effectively as possible. There are obviously different roles involved in achieving this. Everyone, from the managing director, the production manager and technical staff to the supervisors and the machine operatives, has an equal part to play.

The managing director

Responsible for the strategic planning of the business, the managing director should only rarely be involved on the factory floor in times of emergency or significant change to the business, i.e. major changes to the production system or implementation of new production equipment involving significant capital expenditure. But he or she is also responsible for ensuring that the entire team are doing their jobs effectively. The difficulty is that problems can surface weeks and sometimes months afterwards and this has always been a major problem. If there has been a problem that the managing director was unaware of, this may manifest itself through customer complaints and possibly lost orders.

The knock-on effect will be that the production manager is pulled into the managing director's office for a major telling off and everybody within the organisation feels a large element of stress which could have been avoided.

The production manager

He or she is responsible for the day-to-day running and performance of the production floor, including production planning and dealing with problems that arise such as employee discipline and line balancing. Maintaining a disciplined production environment is a vital part of the production manager's job. The supervisors are directly responsible to him or her and should be accountable for their own production lines. This is a very important position, which can also be very stressful, so it is paramount that production managers are given the freedom and support to function to the best of their ability.

The supervisor

Supervisors are responsible for the day-to-day running of their production lines and for setting up the sewing line for new styles of products. Again, this is a very important position because they are in direct contact with the machinists and should be able to pick up problems more quickly because of this. They ensure that production is flowing smoothly and are involved in work progress chasing as well as being a vital element in ensuring that the standards of quality are maintained.

In addition to this supervisors should:

- inspect to see that the operators perform their maintenance duties;
- make sure the machines are properly threaded with the correct thread;
- make sure proper size and type of needles are provided;

- dispose of all broken needles (they should not be left by the machine);
- make sure that all safety procedures are followed.

The garment technologist
This member of the team is responsible for:

- garment development;
- production problems arising from difficult-to-handle fabrics or sewing problems encountered during production;
- setting and accepting standards as agreed by the production manager;
- liaising with supervisors, clothing engineers, production managers and the design team – good communication skills are vital.

The quality assurance inspector
In smaller businesses, the roles of the quality insurance inspector and the garment technologist can be combined. The quality insurance inspector's responsibilities are:

- to ensure that the operators' work matches that set by the standard;
- to bring any associated problems to the attention of the person responsible.

Clothing machine engineers
Machine engineers are sometimes called upon to perform miracles in order to sew the clothing product of the day. Their responsibilities are:

- to set the machines and equipment to the standards agreed by the garment technologist and the production manager;
- to maintain the machines and equipment;
- to make sure that operators perform their daily maintenance duties properly.

The machine operative
This is the most important person in the factory who creates the wealth by manufacturing the product. It is vital therefore that machine operatives are supported by supervisors and management and trained properly for the manufacturing environment. In particular, they are responsible for:

- checking oil gauges to ensure that the machine has sufficient oil;
- lubricating the machine manually when required;
- removing dust and lint from the sewing area;
- changing needles at least once a day;
- making sure that the work they are doing conforms to the standard that has been set, and if it doesn't reporting it to the supervisor immediately (the operation should be stopped until such time as the machine has been altered or the problem has been rectified);
- cleaning their machine at least once a day (this is particularly important for overlockers).

It should also be impressed that in the event of a machine problem, needles should be changed immediately and the threading of the machine should be checked automatically. An old saying in a factory used to be that if you looked after your machine, the machine would look after you. This is as relevant today as it ever was, because a machine that is poorly maintained will tend to break down more, causing lost revenue to the machinist, poor quality of stitching on the garment and lost production to the company.

Important factors to be taken into account

In addition to the above, there are certain other factors that are important and beneficial to production staff regarding quality of production.

A good knowledge of the machinery used
- construction and mechanical features;
- stitch-forming components;
- machine applications for different types of products;
- machine lubrication systems;
- thread consumption of various machine types;
- common machine adjustments;
- feeding mechanisms employed on machine types;
- comparisons between machine types.

Manufacturing methods
- knowledge of basic machinist skills;
- being able to identify British Standard stitch and seam types;
- knowledge of machine types used in the garment-making industry;
- knowledge of applications of guides, attachments and work aids that are available to enhance machine performance and productivity;
- knowledge of automatic machines – features, abilities and applications
- knowledge of work-handling systems;
- knowledge of ancillary equipment, which includes pressing, packaging and cutting machinery.

Sewing problems
- manufacture and use of the needle including needle types, needle points and definitions;
- problems relating to needle damage on fabrics – causes and prevention;
- thread and fabric problems resulting in machine breakdown;
- seam pucker – causes and prevention.

Knowledge of materials used in clothing and related industries
- characteristics of fibres relevant to sewing threads and fabric yarns:
  - natural and synthetic;
  - staple and continuous filament.

- types of sewing thread and fabric yarn construction:
  - staple-spun and core-spun;
  - Z and S twist;
  - thread and yarn counts;
  - relevant thread and yarn finishes.
- various fabric constructions:
  - woven, knitted and non-woven;
  - mechanical properties and fabric hand characteristics;
  - fabric applications.

Problems arising from faulty work

If a garment is found to be below standard, the following procedures should be implemented:

- The machine should be stopped immediately in order to prevent further inferior work from being processed.
- The supervisor and the garment technologist should be notified immediately.
- If another machine is available, the operator should use this machine to continue production.
- The supervisor and the garment technologist should look at the machine to ascertain the cause of the problem.
- If the supervisor and the garment technician cannot sort out the problem, an action sheet should be filled out highlighting the problem and the action taken to correct it. The supervisor and the technologist should then sign the action sheet.
- If the supervisor or the technologist cannot sort out the problem, the production manager should be informed and collective discussion should take place. When the problem is solved, the production manager will sign the action sheet

Someone once posed the question as to why it was necessary for them to have this type of technical information if they were, for example a production manager, supervisor or work-study officer. The answer is that the more fully these people are versed in technical information from the production floor, the greater will be the chances of solving the problem. Also there is greater communication among all members of the team if all possess this type of knowledge.

Fundamentally, quality should not be sacrificed in the name of production. This is unfortunately, one of the major reasons for large amounts of garments slipping through the net only to come back to haunt the business when rejected by customers. There is no excuse for this, and it can be prevented, but it needs a number of things to happen. It needs dedication and commitment from all concerned and full support from senior management. It also needs perseverance and patience. But the most important characteristic of all that it needs is *courage*.

It takes courage to stop a production line or a machine because of a quality problem. It takes courage to collectively get together, sit down and talk the problem through until a solution is found. Courage is probably one of the most important traits that will enable the team to solve the production problem, with the result that the company will be renowned for producing better quality instead of just higher quantity.

Operation of quality control systems

There is no one system of quality control that is best for all clothing factories, because as Clay and Walley state (5):

'If a thing's worth doing, it's worth doing as well as it's worth doing.'

The relative values involved vary considerably according to the quality orientation of the factory. A producer of 'hit and run' merchandise employs the absolute minimum of quality control systems, whereas the manufacturer supplying major chain stores must operate the entire gamut of quality control procedures.

For the majority of clothing factories, quality control is an in-built function, and some of the principles governing its operation are discussed here.

Quality procedures

A successful quality system should be objective and have a clear focus on ensuring that the information is accurate, reliable and well documented. Objectivity is achieved by using reliable data sources and sound analytical techniques and by having efficient procedures developed by qualified people using proven methods. Most companies have their own quality systems that have been developed in-house by the manufacturing team. These will differ depending upon the organisation, but there will also be many similarities between companies. A brief summary of the types of procedures used is given below.

AQL (aceptable quality limits)

An AQL system focuses on prevention rather than detection and employs measured checks against the 'standard' garment to supplement the final audit.

It is essential that the quality of garments going into finished stock is monitored. While the finished stock audit provides a method of feedback from the customer's perspective, the AQL audit is based on the standard set before beginning production in bulk and is viewed from the garment and style technical specification. An initial audit is carried out by a specific team, with follow-up audits being carried out internally.

The factory manager is responsible for ensuring that there is sufficient finished stock for the audit to take place, the minimum quantity of finished stock being 50 dozen (600) garments. The factory manager is also responsible for ensuring that all subsequent audits are carried out, i.e. all colour/fabric options, and follow-up audits in the event of garments failing to meet the required specification. The results should be formally communicated on the relevant documentation of the quality assurance manager.

Seconds procedures

In an ideal world a reject garment would not exist, but in reality this is not the case and rejects can result from numerous causes such as faulty workmanship or pattern, incorrect cutting and so on. Therefore an efficient, cost-effective method of dealing with seconds has to be implemented.

The thrust of the quality improvement program is focused on the prevention of defects both internally and externally from the suppliers. The aim should be to continuously improve performance. However, there are unfortunately occasions when a less than 100% quality performance results in the need to categorise garments as sub-standard or seconds.

Monitoring the level of seconds allows feedback from the production line. This will highlight problem areas by analysing the faults in categories. The cause of the fault is identified so that operators can respond more quickly to a 'failing' garment and ensure that the fault is repaired so that it can be recovered to a 'perfect'. All personnel involved in production will be made aware of the fault so that efforts to prevent further seconds can be made.

The procedure should be referred to when inducting new employees and should be included in any related continuous improvement initiative to ensure that the procedure is documented, controlled and up to date.

Repairs procedure

Repairs cost time, production and money to an organisation, and again prevention is better than detection. However, in the event of repairs being needed, a procedure such as the one below needs to be in place to deal with it.

* When a repair is found, it will be marked with a cross on a repair ticket.
* The garment must be fully examined before it is returned for repair.
* Any garment sent to the line without being examined will be classed as a bonus fault.
* Any garment sent for repair which, in the opinion of the examiner does not require repairing will be classed as a bonus fault.
* All repair tickets must indicate all faults and where possible the operator's number. Any garment which cannot be identified against an operator must be given to the PCS operator with the appropriate work ticket, to allow action by the line supervisor.
* All garments for repair must be returned to the supervisor, not direct to the production line.
* No garments must be returned to the line without a repair ticket and will not be accepted back to the examination section without the same ticket.
* On acceptance to the production line, it is the responsibility of the line supervisor to ensure that all corrective work has been carried out.
* Any garments not having the correct information or not having been correctly examined will be classified as a bonus fault.
* All garments which are repaired will be returned to the examiner who originally examined the garment.
* The examiner will check the parts of the garment which have been repaired and any subsequent parts which may have been affected. Once checked, an all-over appearance check must be done before accepting the garment as passed.

Broken needles and metal contamination procedures

This type of procedure has become very common and is now widely used in most manufacturing companies worldwide. The cost of litigation to a company could be very severe if a person were to scratch or cut themselves on a broken needle when putting on a garment. Therefore the garment suppliers are made to enforce this policy rigorously or suffer the consequences from the customer.

A typical example of a broken needle policy is given below: The block letters are how it would appear as a notice in the factory.

THE BROKEN NEEDLE AND METAL CONTAMINATION PROCEDURE IS A VERY IMPORTANT PART OF THE COMPANY'S QUALITY POLICY.

NOTE:
THIS IS NON-NEGOTIABLE. IT WILL BE REINFORCED RIGOROUSLY.

OPERATOR RESPONSIBILITES
(1)   **NO** PINS, STAPLES OR OTHER SMALL PIECES OF METAL ARE ALLOWED ON SECTIONS OR SEWING MACHINES AND **NO** NEEDLES EXCEPT THOSE IN USE.
(2)   CLEAN MACHINES DAILY. KEEP WORK PLACE CLEAN AND TIDY.
(3)   PLACE CLOTH UNDER FOOT WHEN NOT IN USE.
(4)   BE AWARE OF QUALITY AT ALL TIMES. CHECK STANDARD DAILY AND PRODUCE WORK OF EQUAL QUALITY TO IT.

BROKEN NEEDLE PROCEDURE
(1)   INFORM SUPERVISOR AND TOGETHER TRY TO FIND ALL PIECES. THE SUPER-VISOR IS TO TAPE ALL THE PIECES TO THE BROKEN NEEDLE SHEET BEFORE ISSUING ANOTHER NEEDLE.
(2)   IF UNABLE TO FIND ALL OF THE PIECES, THE SUPERVISOR WILL ATTACH THE PIECES THAT ARE FOUND TO THE SHEET.
      THE SUPERVISOR WILL THEN ISOLATE ALL THE WORK AROUND THE SEWING MACHINE AND CHECK WITH A METAL DETECTOR. WHILST HE/SHE IS DOING THIS, YOU SHOULD CHECK ANY LITTER BINS AND EMPTY THE CON-TENTS INTO A PLASTIC BAG, WHICH MUST BE PUT IN THE DUSTBIN. IF ALL OF THE NEEDLE PIECES CANNOT BE FOUND, THE SUPERVISOR MUST TAKE THE WORK FROM THE SECTION AND INFORM THE FACTORY MANAGER.

USED NEEDLE REPLACEMENT PROCEDURE
WHEN ROUTINELY CHANGING USED NEEDLES, THE OLD NEEDLE **MUST** BE HANDED BACK TO THE **SUPERVISOR** BEFORE A NEW NEEDLE IS ISSUED.
ON NO ACCOUNT MUST AN OPERATOR APPROACH A MECHANIC FOR NEEDLES.

NEEDLE STORAGE
NEW NEEDLES ARE STORED IN A SECURE LOCKED BOX AND ARE KEPT IN THE PRODUCTION OFFICE.

DOCUMENTATION
ALL DOCUMENTATION IS LOGGED ON THE BROKEN NEEDLE PROCEDURE SHEET.

A LAMINATED CARD IS ATTACHED TO EVERY RELEVANT PIECE OF MACHINERY OUTLINING THIS PROCEDURE TO THE OPERATIVES.

Design

Garment design involves the consideration of many commercial factors. One of the most important is the quality framework of each garment in the collection. This framework has to be built into the garment at the design and sampling stage so as to ensure that it can stand up to the basic quality criteria of the company and its customers. Some aspects of this quality framework are as follows.

Patterns

The design should not require structural weak points in the pattern which would cause the garment to fail during reasonable wear. Design features should not create critical areas which require a great deal of extra attention during production and finishing.

Fabrics and trim

Over the years each clothing company develops its own circle of suppliers and through experience knows the extent to which suppliers can be relied on for the behavioural characteristics of their products. In many cases the suppliers themselves have to be approved by the retail organisations served by the factory.

However, the fashion business is dynamic and every season sees new combinations of cloth and trim. The selection and testing of these materials has to be done very carefully. In this sense testing would also include dry-cleaning and/or washing of trial garments.

Pattern grading

Sizing quality is an integral part of garment quality and patterns should be accurately graded not only for size but also to maintain the design proportions of the garment.

Patterns in general

The garment pattern is the bridge connecting design to production and must also incorporate provisions to ensure garment quality. The accurate marking of grain lines, nip alignments, nips indicating non-standard sewing allowances, etc. are all part of the preparation for quality.

Technology

The question here is whether the factory has the necessary process technology to produce the garments at the required levels of quality. Sampling is the time for joint consultation between the designer and technologists, when they decide whether a particular operation should be changed or eliminated, or special machinery purchased for the purpose.

The factory has to have the technological capability to produce economically and at the right quality levels. The best designs remain just designs if the factory cannot produce the garments efficiently and according to the relevant standards of quality.

Standards

A standard is a specification which sets out the criteria for acceptable quality and covers all the characteristics that can be accurately measured. Specifications can be drawn up to cover raw materials, operations, garment measurements, etc. Each specification includes a plus and minus tolerance to the central measurement and this defines the range within which the quality is acceptable. A specification and tolerance for cloth weight could read:

$$280 \, g/m^2 \pm 12 \, g/m^2$$

The specification and tolerance for a seaming operation could read:

seam width 10 mm ± 0.5 mm

There are two types of specification used in factories:

(1) *General*   These apply to all garments produced by the factory or to specific categories. For example:
   • All garments must have country of origin labels in the designated positions.
   • The nylon bags for individual hanging skirts must be bottom sealed 10 cm below the hem.
(2) *Specific*   These relate to particular factors and cover raw material purchases and all the manufacturing processes including cutting, fusing, sewing, pressing and finishing. In addition, storage and transport conditions are specified so that the garments arrive at the warehouse or shop in mint condition.

Inspection

Where standards exist, inspection routines must be operated to check whether the item or operation meets the specified range of acceptable quality. Inspection procedures can be of one of two types, or a combination of both:

(1) *100% inspection*   This involves the inspection of every single item or operation which has been selected for inspection.
(2) *Sampling*   This is a more sophisticated technique based on the 'Law of Regularity' which states that a sufficiently large sample taken at random will exhibit similar characteristics to the whole group from which it was drawn. There are standard tables which provide the predictive accuracy of a particular sample size in relation to batch size.

For example, if 100 rolls of cloth were received from a mill and the standard sample size for cloth deliveries was 10%, then ten rolls would be taken at random from the delivery and inspected. If the inspection of the sample showed a high fault rate, then another sample would be taken so as to validate or alter the findings of the first random sample. If the second sample corroborated the findings of the first sample, then the entire batch could be rejected or subjected to 100% inspection. Normally the short lead times of the clothing industry do not permit a replacement delivery for rejected merchandise, and a faulty batch is accepted subject to negotiations between the supplier and the factory.

A factory might use random sampling procedures for all the manufacturing processes and 100% inspection for finished garments.

Analysis

The results of the sampling are collated according to the main groups of operation, such as cutting, fusing, sleeve setting, etc., and the findings are recorded on control charts. The chart itself consists of pairs of horizontal lines which represent the following:

- the average range of quality for the process;
- the warning range, which means that results falling in this area call for extra vigilance;
- the action limits which denote that immediate action must be taken if results fall in this area.

A chart of this type indicates general and specific trends and provides factual information for production management to act on. The chart illustrated in Figure 18.3

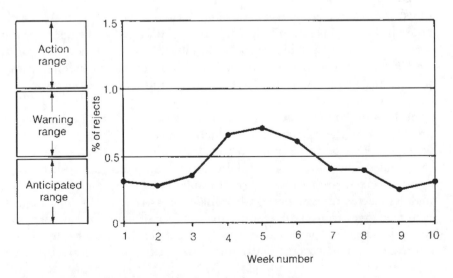

Fig. 18.3 Quality analysis chart for cutting room

In-process quality report						
Name	Number	Operation			Daily norm	Sample size
Linda	4077	306 – Tack pocket			340 Prs.	17–20
Date	Sample	Faulty	Alter	Reject	Comments	Inspector
12/4	18	1	1	–	OK	
13/4	17	2	2	–	OK	
14/4	19	4	2	2	Follow up	
15/4	18	3	1	2	Follow up	
15/4	20	2	2	–	Improved	
15/4	18	1	1	–	Improved	
16/4	17	0	–	–	Good	
16/4	21	1	1	–	OK	
Totals	148	14	10	4	Quality Rating	97

Fig. 18.4 Operator quality report

shows the overall quality performance of the cutting room over a given period of time.

Reporting

The types of report used and their frequency vary from factory to factory but they are all based on the same principles.

(1) *Operator reports* In-process inspection records the results of the samples taken from each operation (Fig. 18.4) and shows whether the operator is performing at an acceptable or below-standard level. In the event of substandard work, remedial action is taken by the supervisor and/or the inspector and the frequency of inspection is stepped up until the operator reaches and consistently maintains the required standards.

In the more sophisticated types of incentive scheme, operator quality levels are a factor in the calculation of premium payments.

(2) *Management reports* Reports of this nature present an overall picture of the total quality levels achieved by the factory during a specific period. They also compare past and current results in order to establish trends and highlight actual and/or potential problem areas (Fig. 18.5). One important factor emerges from these reports: the number of Grade A garments out of the total quantity produced during a given period. This figure is usually expressed as a percentage and is used as a criterion for evaluating quality performance.

										Week no. 6	
		Quality report									
Style number	Quantity	Cutting	Fusing	Sewing 'A'	Sewing 'B'	Pressing	Finishing	Stains	Damages	Total rejects	% of quantity
7118	1210	4		2	3		1	3	14	27	2.23
7491	870			4	2		1	1	7	15	1.72
7168	220			1	1	1		1	2	6	2.73
7216	450		1		2		1	1	5	10	2.22
7219	650	1			3			2	9	15	2.31
Total	3,400	5	1	7	11	1	3	8	37	73	2.15
% of total		0.15	0.03	0.20	0.32	0.03	0.09	0.23	1.09		
To date	17,100	0.17	0.03	0.18	0.32	0.03	0.14	0.24	1.06	371	2.17
Trends % increase				11.1					2.8		
Trends % decrease	11.7						35.7	4.1		1.62	0.92

Fig. 18.5 Management report on quality

To sum up

Garment technology is concerned with deciding which materials and processes are required to achieve specified levels of garment quality. Inspection verifies whether these levels are being reached and maintained. Quality procedures are therefore the control function of technological planning.

Bibliography

1. Blackburn J.A. (1969) *Management in the Textile Industry*. The Textile Institute – Longmans, London.
2. Business Monitor (BM) PA 1002 (1996) Table 5 [O.N.S. (1996) P.A. 1002 *Manufacturing – Summary Volume*. HMSO, London] in Jones R.M. (2002) *The Apparel Industry*. Blackwell Science Ltd, Oxford.
3. Carr H. & Latham B. (1988) *The Technology of Clothing Manufacture*. BSP Professional Books, Oxford.
4. Chuter A.J. (1988) *Introduction to Clothing Production Management*. BSP Professional Books, Oxford.
5. Clay M.J. & Walley B.H. (1985) *Performance and Profitability*. Longmans, London.
6. Coats J.P. (undated) *The Technology of Thread and Seams*. J. & P. Coats Ltd, Glasgow.
7. Coleridge N. (1989) *The Fashion Conspiracy*. William Heinemann, London.
8. Cooklin G. (1989) *Fusing Technology*. The Textile Institute, Manchester.
9. Cooklin G. (1990) *Cutting Room Technology*. The Ministry of Labour, Jerusalem.
10. Currie R.M. (1967) *Work Study*. Sir Isaac Pitman Ltd, London.
11. Currie R.M. (1965) *Financial Incentives*. British Institute of Management, London.
12. Drucker P. (1968) *The Practice of Management*. Pan Books, London.
13. Evans G.R. & Berman B. (1982) *Marketing*. Macmillan Publishing Inc., New York.
14. Bertrand Frank Associates (1982) *Profitable Merchandising of Apparel*. National Knitwear and Sportswear Association, New York.
15. Friend R.L. (1977) *Sewing Room Technical Handbook*. HATRA, The Research Centre for Knitting, Dyeing and Making-up, Nottingham.
16. Gaetan M. (1977) *Sewn Products Engineering*. Bobbin Publications, Columbia, South Carolina.
17. Hudson P.B. (1989) *Guide to Apparel Manufacturing*. Mediapparel Inc., North Carolina.
18. Hunter N.A. (1990) *Quick Response in Apparel Manufacturing*. The Textile Institute, Manchester.
19. Johnson-Hill B. (1978) *Fashion Your Future*. The Clothing Institute, England.
20. Koontz H. & O'Donnell C. (1964) *Principles of Management*. McGraw-Hill, New York.
21. Lowe J. and Lowcock P.D. (1986) *An Approach to Quality Control in the Clothing Industry*. Emraine Publications, Herts.
22. McGregor D. (1983) *The Human Side of Enterprise*. McGraw-Hill, New York.
23. NEDO National Economic Development Office (1968) *Figures Help*. HMSO, London.
24. NEDO (undated) *Recruitment Selection and Training*. HMSO, London.
25. NEDO (1971) *Technology and the Garment Industry*. HMSO, London.
26. NEDO (1971) *Work Study in the Clothing Industry*. HMSO, London.
27. Pugh T.M. (1987) *Garment Engineering*. The Clothing and Footwear Institute, London.
28. Rae A. (1964) *Work Study*. Odhams Books Ltd, London.

29. Schierbaum W. (1982) *Bekleidungs Lexikon*. Schiele and Schön, Berlin.
30. Sizer L. (1969) *An Insight into Management Accounting*. Penguin Books, Harmondsworth, Middlesex.
31. Stapleton J. (1989) *How to Prepare a Marketing Plan*. Gower Publishing Ltd., London.
32. Stohlman D. (1969) The Quality Control Manual. *Bobbin Journal*, May and June, Columbia, South Carolina.
33. Taylor P. (1990) *Computers in the Fashion Industry*. Heinemann Professional Publishing, Oxford.
34. Wilson J.R. (1986) *The UK Fashion Designer Scene*. Department of Trade and Industry, London.

Index

Printed and bound in the UK by
CPI Antony Rowe, Eastbourne